W9-BHE-026

Mastering the News Media Interview

Mastering the News Media Interview

How to Succeed
at Television, Radio,
and Print Interviews

Stephen C. Rafe

 HarperBusiness
A Division of HarperCollins*Publishers*

Library of Congress Cataloging-in-Publication Data

Rafe, Stephen C.
  Mastering the news media interview : how to succeed at television,
radio, and print interviews / Stephen C. Rafe.
     p. cm.
  Includes bibliographical references and index.
  ISBN 0-88730-439-7
  1. Interviewing in journalism.   I. Title.
PN4784.I6R34   1991
070.4'3—dc20   91-13683
                                                               CIP

Designed by Joan Greenfield

Copyright © 1991 by Stephen C. Rafe. All rights reserved. No part of this publication may be reproduced, stored in a retrieval system, or transmitted in any form or by any means, electronic, mechanical, photocopy, recording, or otherwise without the prior written consent of the author.

PRINTED IN THE UNITED STATES OF AMERICA

91 92 93 94 CC/HC 9 8 7 6 5 4 3 2 1

To my clients, who are willing to try new concepts as I develop them from leading-edge research in the field of communication into practical applications they can use in their careers.

You help to prove that the best people in any endeavor strive to become even better at whatever challenges them—and succeed.

Contents

Part Three: The Interview

Part Four: Other Types of Interviews

Foreword

Television stories, like their counterparts in print, once had a distinct beginning, middle, and end. This is no longer the case. A television story used to be linear: new information was piled on the old as the story progressed through its allotted time. Today, however, a well-structured television story is more likely to be holographic or spherical than strictly linear.

As in a holograph, where the entire database or image is present in every part of the transmitting medium, the essence of a television story is apparent at every point during the piece. Additional time in today's television story adds clarity and resolution, not substantive information.

Some might criticize this approach to delivering information as shallow, but it is hard to argue against its effectiveness. After all, conveying the clearest possible picture of an issue or event in the shortest possible time should be the communicator's highest goal.

The power of television resides partly in its ability to extend our field of vision and let us experience places and events that would otherwise be inaccessible. But television is also remarkable for its ability to clarify and enhance the resolution of images and ideas at a deep level of consciousness—deeper than words.

I once heard Shad Northshield say when he was executive producer of "CBS Sunday Morning" that he received letters almost every week asking for the text of the poetry that was read under the nature video that closed the show. Those sequences are always run with natural sound; no words, poetry or prose, have ever intruded. But the overall impression the images convey is so strong, so elemental, that many viewers simply assume that they are being spoken to.

They are being told something, of course. They are being delivered an image, an idea, that resonates deeply in their minds. They are responding to the kind of impressionistic information that television is uniquely capable of delivering.

David Bartlett, President
Radio-Television News
Directors Association, Inc.

Preface

This is my third book with HarperBusiness on my methods and techniques for preparing managers, professionals, executives, scientists, researchers, and technicians at all levels to face audiences and handle interviews successfully. Readers of the first two books have told me that having access to this much information about my methods is a relatively inexpensive way to learn most of what clients pay me handsomely to teach them. In fact, the only thing that this book does not provide is the opportunity to work directly with them on points related to individual needs and issues. Individual guidance in bringing out your personal best has to be accomplished in seminars and coaching sessions.

Otherwise, this book tells it all. It is packed with information you can use immediately to handle news-media interviews and appearances, whether you are about to face your first one or have been through several and simply want to improve your skills.

Some of the concepts discussed in this book also can be found in one or both of my other books. This is inevitable since my best advice and many general principles apply in many communications environments. Even where material may seem familiar, however, the applications are different.

Adults learn best when they receive information in sequential and cumulative fashion and mark their progress from one unit to the next, so this book has been structured accordingly. Before you apply any of the techniques you discover here to a given situation, I encourage you to read the book from cover to cover. Although there are no absolutes in handling media interviews and appearances, you will do best if you have an overview of the many tried-and-true techniques that make the task more enjoyable. This book attempts to cover all these techniques, but to the extent that it may not, I invite you to write to me with any questions or areas that you feel need to be addressed.

Thousands have followed the advice presented in this book to succeed in an area that even communications professionals sometimes find difficult. In fact, many who did not do well in media interviews before coming to me have gone on to actually welcome media interviews and appearances.

Whether you need to interact with the media in crisis situations, appear on talk shows, make audiotapes or videotapes, or participate in teleconferences, the techniques you will discover here can help you as they have helped thousands of spokespersons in major corporations, associations, government, politics, and religious organizations throughout the world.

Introduction

If you want to succeed when you are interviewed by the news media, you need specific, tangible, concrete information about how to prepare your *self* and your *subject* to deal with the interview *situations* that you encounter. This book provides that information and more.

U.S. presidents and other heads of state, as well as leaders from all other walks of life, are coached for dealing with the news media. They are taken through mock interviews and even full-scale news conferences that can sometimes be more challenging than the real thing. The principal objective of all such sessions is to help spokespersons understand the media's needs and rules, become comfortable with the interview process, develop a willingness to speak for their organizations, and acquire the skills needed to communicate the content portion of their message clearly, concisely, and with total credibility. When that has been accomplished, the public's interest is served.

More often than not, our attitudes toward news-media professionals are influenced by their responses to our attitudes toward them. It's the old story: expect trouble and look for it, and you'll probably find it.

An instructive story tells about a married couple who left a real estate office, approached an older man seated on a park bench, and asked him about the kind of community he lived in. The older man responded with a question: "What was the town like where you're coming from?"

"Oh," groaned the husband, "we can't wait to move. The neighbors were backstabbing social climbers. The whole atmosphere was negative and even hostile. We're ready to get out of there."

"Well," sighed the older man, "you'll probably find all that here, too."

The two went on, and a little later another couple walked out of the same real estate office and over to the same man sitting on the same park bench. "Excuse me," one of the two said politely, "Would you mind telling us what kind of community this is?"

"Sure," said the older man. "What was the town like where you're coming from?"

"Oh, we're going to miss it," the wife said nostalgically. "Some of the best people I've ever known," the husband chimed in. "Yes," said one as the other nodded, "such kindness, such caring, such consideration. We've had good friends there."

"Well," the older man said with a twinkle as he shifted forward on the bench, "you'll probably find the same kind of people here."

Why not anticipate having positive relationships with your contacts with the news media? Why not learn how the game is played and how to take charge of yourself, your subject, and the situations in which you are likely to be interviewed? Why not learn to do this so well that you can help produce win-win outcomes for all parties? Once you establish rapport with interviewers, you can recognize a mutual need to do a job and to approach problems from different perspectives.

Don't expect reporters and interviewers to become your friends, however—at least not to the extent of being your confidants. Many prefer to maintain a certain distance, perhaps to work objectively and have the public acknowledge that objectivity.

Much of today's reporting—even print journalism—is influenced by television's ability to provide instant coverage of fast-breaking stories. Television appeals to both the auditory and visual senses of its audiences much more intensely than newspapers and magazines do to theirs, but television has less permanency or "recall-ability" than print media, and radio has even less. Stories in last week's newspaper or magazine are still readily available, but most people don't keep transcripts or videotapes of every television or radio news program, talk show, or interview.

Despite these disadvantages television establishes today's standards for most news reporting and interviewing, and as David Bartlett's foreword to this book suggests, television brings us clear impressions of issues and events in a short time. As we recognize and accept television's limitations and appreciate its strengths, we can better equip our-

---

TIME IS MONEY

In electronic journalism, minutes translate directly into dollars. For some years now, broadcasters have been using such high-tech equipment as Lexicon time-compression units to speed up movies and old programs for reruns. The reason? Shave as little as 8 to 10 percent of the total running time from each program and the station adds thousands of dollars per program in potential advertising revenues. Time is money, indeed.

---

selves to survive news-media interviews and also help those interviews achieve positive outcomes for all concerned.

The electronic and print media require income to do their job, and most of that income comes from support funds or commercial advertising (see box). There is a fine line between generating income and producing quality programming, but ultimately, the public chooses what it will read, listen to, or watch. Sitcoms and soaps are on the air only because the public allows them to be, and the same is true for the talk shows, news programs, feature articles, and news stories in which you may find yourself participating.

This book does not discuss the important issues of integrity, morals, or ethics. It focuses on only one objective: helping you master news-media interviews so that all concerned emerge as winners. Because television establishes the standards for all communication in today's society and requires more skills of its interview subjects than radio or print media do, those skills are the primary topics examined in these pages.

Mastering the News Media Interview

Part One
Interviews and the News Media

1
Understanding the News Media's Role

"Why do the news media always pick the worst possible times to show up?" a company executive exclaimed in one of our seminars. Certainly many executives feel that newspaper, radio, and television reporters often arrive on the scene when they may not be at their best. There are the reporters—at a zoning change request hearing, an environmental issues meeting, a presentation on why a plant should be allowed to expand, or even at corporate headquarters in the center of a major crisis (see box).

In many cases, reporters work against deadlines, so they rush in, ask questions, take notes, and then head out the door to file the story, leaving as quickly as they arrived.

As you watch the six o'clock news that evening, or as you turn to the next morning's paper, you may see a report that bears little resemblance to what you felt took place. The story may not contain any falsehoods, but it emphasizes and omits facts that put it in a context entirely different from what you think is appropriate. It may report what you also saw, heard, or said but somehow differently than you remember the exchange.

The Role of Conflict

Reporters know that conflict sells newspapers and keeps audiences tuned in. When conflict and drama in a story must be emphasized in the brief amount of space or time allocated, differences in perspective occur.

MEDIA APPEARANCES —
THREATS, CHALLENGES, OR OPPORTUNITIES

Mitchell P. Davis, President, Broadcast Interview Source, Washington, DC

This country publishes nearly 1,650 daily newspapers and some 50,000 newsletters. The U.S. and Canada combined publish more than 65,000 periodicals. The United States alone has more than 1,000 television stations, 4,700 AM radio stations, and 4,400 FM radio stations.

If you are not prepared to handle media appearances, you may feel intimidated by these numbers and perceive them as threats or challenges. However, for those who know the rules and can play the game, they represent a force for communicating your messages more powerful than the world has ever known.

Even reporters feel frustrated with the process when they are in a situation where they have no time to research a story in depth or to report it thoroughly. In the first sentence or two of their story, they must report the answers to the standard journalistic questions—who, what, when, where, why, and how. Even these answers are likely to be reduced to the most dramatic ("newsworthy") statements possible in order to hook the sustained attention of the reader, listener, or viewer.

Because it is easier to find the conflict hook in bad news than it is to find it in so-called good-news stories, reporters often report the negative aspects of events. This is not necessarily biased reporting; it is a practicality, given the pressure of deadlines. The facts and details a reporter selects are those that emphasize or dramatize the points of conflict he or she feels are integral to the story. When the reporter perceives himself or herself as an advocate for the "little guy" and you are not that person, you may not like the way the story is covered.

How the Media Vary

Reporters for newspapers and magazines look for data that support their concept of conflict and seek out reports and documents that can be excerpted and officials who can be asked questions that elicit meaty, quotable statements. Radio reporters try for the on-the-scenes quotes that bring immediacy to their coverage and sometimes use aggressive questioning techniques and loaded or leading questions as they press for responses. Television reporters also need immediacy, and they look for 30-second quotes that can be accompanied by visual drama—fires, the scene in front of the courthouse, and so on.

What an Organization Can Do

The opportunities for radio, television, and newspaper coverage are expanding, but so is the competition for the time and space. More groups seek air time and print space, and more stations scramble for their share of the action.

As Alvin Toeffler predicted many years ago in *Future Shock*, we have entered an era of acceleration and diversity. Nowhere is this more pronounced than in the media's treatment of the news. When the media reduce a one-hour interview to three sentences that make the airwaves, something is bound to be lost in that effort to cover even more stories.

Organizations must prepare executives for the possibility of news coverage. In this era, anyone can be in front of a camera without warning, and being on the firing line unprepared can place jobs in jeopardy.

Every executive in every career needs to know and understand the techniques required for dealing successfully with the news media. They need to understand reporters' styles, techniques, and news formats. If the Mike Wallaces of journalism can spend entire careers preparing to interview executives, the executives should certainly spend a few hours learning about the news media.

It is no longer possible to avoid negative media exposure by ducking reporters who seek the story. As many organizations have learned the hard way, an uncooperative attitude simply keeps the pot boiling and forces reporters to seek the story elsewhere—prehaps from someone with an axe to grind. If an organization does not do its own talking, some other group may do it for them—and the results could be chaotic. The same holds true for the "no comment" answer once an interview has begun. When one executive gave a television interviewer a "no comment" answer, the reporter thrust back by saying: "Sir, I must assume, then, by your 'no comment' answer, that your company is guilty."

How to Help Channel Conflict

Since interviews are here to stay, organizations should be prepared for them and learn how to channel a reporter's need for conflict into positive directions. One way to do this is to point out the counterarguments to a critic's charges.

Consider the following illustration. A manufacturing plant plans to develop a new road to route its heavy vehicles away from neighborhood traffic. The company is willing to finance and construct the short section of road at no cost to the community. If local opponents succeed in blocking the needed approvals, they could force the company to continue to run heavy vehicles on a road that now passes a recently constructed elementary school and through areas in which traffic is increasing.

To introduce the company's valid motives for building the road and provide a perspective on the issue that the news media should consider, a company spokesperson might ask reporters to consider whether those who oppose the road are acting in the public's interest. Such a question, unemotionally phrased, raises a point that most reporters would pursue in the interest of balanced journalism.

Get to Know Reporters

The first step in influencing how conflict is be reported is to know regular reporters and their assignment editors. They are human, with good days and bad, preferences and prejudices, likes and dislikes. They also try to be objective and unbiased in their approach to a story.

Address their professionalism, fairness, and accuracy. Indicate that you expect not favoritism but fair treatment. Then make yourself available so that they can cover your side of the story—even if it is a negative story—in time for deadline.

Try to empathize with reporters' needs and priorities. Ask them about deadlines, how stories are assigned, how you can take the initiative in getting a particular story told. Ask how stories are rewritten or edited. Find out who writes those headlines—usually not the reporter—that catch the reader's eye but may empasize aspects of the story that you would prefer to see in small type.

You also might try to learn how the reporter feels about the way his or her station or paper treats news coverage. Ask what his or her career goals and aspirations are. Find out how he or she trained for the job. Ask what puts a story on page one.

There are dozens of questions you can raise that show your interest in learning more about the people who cover your stories and the process each story goes through. If you talk with reporters and editors when a story is not at stake, you both will communicate better under pressure.

Don't hesitate to ask for the reporter's views on your operations. Where does he or she feel improvements could be made? When you ask, however, be prepared to research the reporter's suggestions and then respond. In one instance, a reporter pinpointed an employee turnover problem and gave the plant manager some specific approaches to solving it. The suggestions worked, and everyone profited.

When you are courteous and cooperative instead of antagonistic and defensive, reporters are more likely to hear and understand your viewpoints when you tell your story—and give you opportunities to express your point of view when others accuse your organization of misdeeds.

What You Can Expect

Reporters will grill you when they are on the trail of a big story, and you should expect that to happen. Nevertheless, unpleasant experiences can be made more palatable if you know each other and are committed to treating each other fairly.

A newspaper editor once questioned me for 20 minutes at the scene of a plant accident, filed his story, then spent the next several hours on the telephone helping me correct erroneous information other journalists were receiving from an outside source. When the story made page one headlines, it was reported fairly and accurately. The editor's concern for accuracy was a major factor in the story's effectiveness, but equally important was my cooperation. Because the story was reported completely, the paper did not need to run a series of festering stories over several days. Ducking from the press does not make a story go away: it sends resentful reporters to try to pry the story piece by piece from other, often less reliable, sources.

Your Obligations

As a spokesperson for your organization you are in the limelight at times when you would prefer anonymity. Every remark before an audience becomes fair game for a news story. Reporters also may seek out your viewpoints on issues that may be only remotely related to your operations. This is the tradeoff for good media relations.

However, the more you cooperate with reporters, the more likely they will seek out and report your organization's side of a story whenever conflict occurs. When that happens, your constructive input can help shape the story. Meet them. Return their phone calls. Respect their rights to exclusive stories they have developed. Treat them equally when you initiate a story. Tell the truth. Don't attempt to talk "off the record." Never hide behind technical jargon and excuses. Neither give, nor expect, favoritism.

Strive for mutual understanding and respect, and you will have a better chance of having your side of any story told fairly and accurately.

2
Interviews and Their Implications

Middle and upper-level management executives, as well as scientific and technical professionals, increasingly find themselves on television. Cable, teleconferencing, internal programs, videotaped training programs, as well as local and network news programs are a reality, and all rely on interviews. Each kind of exposure has its own risks for the unprepared, but the television news interview offers the greatest risk.

Why You Should Prepare

Top interviewers spend entire careers preparing for your executives. It certainly is advisable for executives to spend a few hours, at least, preparing for those interviewers.

With proper preparation, most television interviews are positive, rewarding experiences. In fact, 90 percent of interviews are nonthreatening. There is always the chance that one or two may fall within the other 10 percent, however, so it helps to understand what makes the news media tick.

VISUAL INTEREST
For starters, television interviewers need a story that lends itself to visual interest. After all, television is a medium that depends upon pictures that move and convey meaning. This cannot be gained from the still photos used in the print media. When that element is missing from your television interview, you have to work harder to create mental

9

pictures for the audience. There is nothing more boring than what television describes as a "talking head."

DRAMA AND CONFLICT

Television journalists have a tough job to do. In a couple of hundred words, they have to tell a news story that describes who, what, when, where, why, and how and that hooks the viewer to continue watching. To do this requires drama and conflict.

Where do these ingredients come from? News programs report a preponderance of stories that are based on negative drama and negative conflict because they are readily available and also because larger audiences have been shown to be attracted to negative stories than to positive ones. Since negative events in 45-second clips keep people tuned in, television brings them to its audience.

It is, and will always be, your job to provide positive drama and constructive conflict. For example, in a bad-news situation, directly address what has happened, then let the news media know what you are doing *right* about the situation—to rectify it and prevent it from happening again, for example. Do this in the most dramatic way possible. Don't drag your feet when bad news strikes and then expect to be able to come from behind when others make accusations and speculate over what you should or should not have done. Consider the *Valdez* oil spill, for example. The media's coverage portrayed a company that was passive and defensive rather than active and concerned. How you should respond to the news media in a crisis is covered in chapter 14.

RATINGS AND REPUTATIONS

Many people identify with the television interviewers they watch, and interviewers are acutely aware that their ratings and reputation are critical to the success of their careers. Their role in relationship to their audiences is to always appear to come out on top in an interview confrontation. To do this they often place the interviewee in stressful situations, to which the "guest" responds in three inappropriate ways: by fight (and anger often plays right into the reporter's hand), fright (which inspires some reporters to intimidate even more), or flight (and if you walk out of an interview, you lose).

When you want to strike verbally at a reporter, attack only the issue. Through proper rehearsal and coaching, you can discover that you are in complete charge of yourself and your answers. No one can make you angry. No one can make you defensive. No one can put words in your mouth. The interviewer can do only what you allow to be done. Even when the interview turns negative, respond with a calm, courteous, and cooperative attitude. Reporters use several identifiable techniques to evoke positive or negative responses in their interviewees, and these techniques, and how you should handle them, are discussed in parts 3 and 4 of this book.

The Right Attitude

As an interview guest, your most valuable asset is your attitude. Your position should be that "we are all in this together" and that people in the audience are your friends. To do this, you need to find as many areas of agreement with the reporter and his or her audience as possible. If asked about your company's concern for water quality, you might say, "Of course we want clean water. My kids and many children of people who are watching today all swim in that water." This establishes rapport with the audience and a collaborative rather than adversarial relationship with the interviewer.

BE ENTERTAINING
Audiences expect to be entertained when they watch television. Think about who watches television, particularly daytime programs—pensioners, shift workers, housekeepers, sick people, vacationers, unemployed. They certainly don't want to watch a spokesperson sitting stiffly with arms glued to his or her sides and drily making polysyllabic pronouncements. They want to be entertained. No career-minded interviewer can afford to allow a spokesperson to drone on in dull and pedantic phrases. He or she must keep the interview interesting. Interviewees either must be entertaining or risk being used as entertainment (see boxes).

CONQUERING "MIKE" FRIGHT
I actually enjoyed my interview with Mike Wallace on "60 Minutes." It demonstrates that win-win methods work even under what some consider the most difficult test of all.

Before my former partner and I were interviewed by Mike Wallace on "60 Minutes" about our spokesperson-coaching business, we met with the executive producer, Grace Diekhaus. Our objective was to understand each other's needs for a good segment and to provide interesting and informative responses to Wallace's questions. These meet-

YOUR RIGHTS IN A SPONTANEOUS INTERVIEW

- To know who is interviewing you and whom he or she represents.
- To have both parties agree on the ground rules, no matter how hastily arranged.
- To be treated courteously. The questions can be tough, but the reporter should not be abusive.
- To have off-the-record comments (which should be kept to a minimum) respected as such and not used in any context.
- To have microphones, lights, and cameras kept at a reasonable distance from you during the interview.
- To keep reporters away from dangerous areas during a crisis.
- To have reporters pool their coverage when necessary to limit the number of people in an area during an emergency.
- To end the interview after a reasonable amount of time, but only after the important questions have been answered.

ings helped us anticipate almost every question we were asked—some verbatim—during the three-hour filming session (of which only a couple of minutes were shown on the air). Our rehearsals were the key to our ability to provide Wallace with material that "played."

For example, we knew that Wallace was aware of the growing controversy about the blurring distinction between news and entertainment in interview programming and that it interested him as a veteran journalist. Our material on this issue worked well and was used on the air. It also gave one of our clients an opportunity to be seen in top form on "60 Minutes" in a segment that showed our client in complete control during a heated moment that originally aired on the "Donahue" show.

Other spokesperson coaches who were interviewed on this "60 Minutes" segment had their own videotape crews tape everything Wallace's crew filmed or did. Instead of regarding the interview as a confrontational experience and feeling the need to ensure accuracy of reporting, throughout our negotiations and in our prefilm briefing with Wallace, we said only what we chose to say and in a way that could be used only in context, we were prepared to establish good rapport with Wallace, we knew we actually would enjoy the experience, and we knew we could contribute something constructive to the segment.

Our positive attitudes paid off: we were treated fairly, honestly, and openly. Although some of the other interviewees were recorded on

YOUR RIGHTS IN PREARRANGED INTERVIEWS (OFFICE OR STUDIO)

- To enjoy all the rights you have in a spontaneous interview.
- To know the issues, subject, or general direction of the interview so you can prepare properly.
- To know approximately how long the interview will last.
- To know whether others will appear with you on a talk show or panel discussion and what their role will be.
- To have a public-relations person or other company representative present.
- To make your own audiotape or videotape of the interview or obtain a complete tape from the station.
- To be recorded only when advised. Preinterview discussions, talk between commercials, or postshow conversations should not be used without your approval.
- To be physically comfortable while the interview is conducted. This includes an appropriate setting, chair, makeup, and so on, with the cooperation of the director and the floor manager.
- To have prerecorded answers remain intact with their essential message when aired.
- To have your interview properly prefaced on the air.
- To be allowed to answer without interruptions, assuming your answers are brief and to the point.
- To ignore editorial comments or negative asides by interviewers or panelists.
- To have the opportunity to make some of your points and not to be limited to programmed responses.

location where lighting was unflattering, our segment was taped in a CBS studio with full studio lighting. Diekhaus and Wallace were professionals at all times and did their jobs well. So did we.

FACING THE ISSUES

Every reporter covers the who, what, when, where, and why of every story. In newspapers these elements customarily are found in the opening, or lead, paragraph of a news story, and then the rest of the piece amplifies these details as space and advertising revenues to pay for that space allow. On radio and television the same news story may not get beyond the first-paragraph details. Feature stories, whether broadcast or printed, usually are based on interviews and tend to open with a grabber—a lead paragraph or statement that entices the readers, listener, or viewer to become involved with the story.

Reporters and interviewers need to convey this information to do their jobs, but readers, listeners, or viewers first must want to pay attention to the story. Journalists develop a sense of what their audiences want and need from them.

WHAT'S LEFT UNSPOKEN

Audiences have other, unspoken questions that reporters must answer to keep them attentive. The unspoken questions are "So what? Who cares? What's in it for me?" The audience wants to know the answers to their hidden questions, which include, "Why are you telling me this? Why should I want to pay attention? How will listening to you make my life (job, etc.) better?"

Get to Know Your Audience   You should learn as much as you can about the people who will read, hear, or see what you have to say. You want to know who they are in terms of age, location, politics, family status, incomes, social levels, educational background, occupation, and knowledge of, interest in, and opinions on your topic. In short, develop a complete demographic profile for the geographical area covered and the socioeconomic background of those most likely to receive your message. This research is imperative when your business is located in the community served by these media. When you formulate statements for interviews, address the audience's needs and interests. The more you can do to understand the media's audiences and prepare yourself accordingly, the more likely you are to succeed.

Start with Understanding   Understanding your interviewer's audience is an important step in determining how you are going to phrase the statements you plan to make. You can remain true to your principles and convictions while addressing the varying points of view represented by a multitude of potential audiences.

If you plan to reduce the number of employees at a given location, for example, you need to determine the issues that concern organized labor, the Chamber of Commerce, the school board, environmental action groups, and so on and select the one that is most important to your cause. Announcing a plant closing that eliminates 500 employees could have the union stampeding your doors, the environmentalists cheering in the streets, and the Chamber and school board wondering where their income is going to come from next year. It might be possible for some to please all the people all the time on some issues, but a more realistic approach is to know whom you're going to gain or lose if you emphasize a particular aspect.

Address the Issues   When you communicate your messages, you should address the concerns of various interest groups. Relate your points to their interests, explain how your goals or actions will affect them, outline the steps they can take to achieve certain outcomes, and tell them how to measure your statements in terms of their own expectations and success.

- *Relate your points to their interests*   Speak in terms that you have previously determined will reflect their positions on the issue at hand during your interviews.
- *Explain how your goals or actions will affect them*   Talk about this from both long-term and short-term perspectives. Discuss lifestyle and pocketbook.
- *Outline the steps they can take to achieve certain outcomes*   Tell them how to respond to your message—actions to take and even how to think and feel about what you have said.
- *Tell them how to measure your statements in terms of their own expectations and success*   Let them know that you will provide some of what they want and need. If you say that jobs will be gradually eliminated and the job market will absorb everyone who is laid off, explain how this will happen and offer proof that the market can, indeed, accommodate everyone.

To communicate your message effectively, you need to do your homework. Your analysis of any major issue always should be performed long before the topic comes to journalists' attention.

3
Television and an Era of Instant Everything

Television sets the standards for how we communicate—how we pace ourselves, pay attention, ask questions and respond to them, and evaluate others. Because television audiences look for entertainment and not just information, those needs must be balanced in a way that does not sacrifice the integrity, morals, or ethics of journalists or their audiences. As television networks pursue both ratings and reputations, they will continue to exploit personality. Television is a medium of impressions: the people you see on your home screens communicate by their postures, facial expressions, and body language before they say a word (see box).

During one of the televised presidential debates in 1980, I was doing a workshop in Atlanta, Georgia, home state of then President Jimmy Carter. Toward the end of the day, we asked workshop participants to watch and prepare to discuss the presidential debate between Carter and Reagan. As soon as it concluded and before reporter commentary

---

IMPACT OF YOUR DELIVERY ON AN AUDIENCE
Albert T. Mehrabian

    7% is content.
    38% is voice.
    55% is nonverbals.

---

began, the group was asked, "What do you recall about what Carter or Reagan said?" When they hesitated and then began to comment on their impressions of the debaters, I asked for content and waited for another response. Finally, and with some coaching, one participant recalled that Reagan said, "There you go again, Mr. President." After still more prompting, someone else recalled that Carter had implied that his young daughter, Amy, was his nuclear advisor.

Less than two minutes after a debate between candidates for the highest elective office in this country, the executives in the workshop could remember nothing about the issues discussed or the positions of each candidate on those issues. They could remember only impressions.

Television's influence in today's society has extended beyond the tube. It has become the standard by which we assess others. We are increasingly concerned with

- *Pace*   People want things to happen quickly: so little time, so much to do.
- *Attention span*   The ability to concentrate on a single topic for long periods has dropped dramatically. It even has affected the clergy: preachers tell me they have cut their sermons from an average of 60 minutes to about 15 over the past couple of decades.
- *Asking and responding to questions*   The ability to ask and answer questions has been raised as people see effective interviews conducted on television. In the long run, society may benefit from this because more issues are raised and explored in greater depth.
- *Alertness to manipulation*   People who learn probing skills from sophisticated media interviewers are unlikely to be duped by those techniques. Misuse of these techniques, however, can, and sometimes does, result in unfair manipulation of others who are unskilled in such matters.
- *Evaluating others*   Sizing up other people at a glance is something else we have learned from television. In an era of instant assessments, making quick judgments is hard to resist.
- *Personal styles*   Values and styles change through the powerful effect of modeling. As audiences watch people on television, they are influenced by television's ability to spotlight, and even create, trends.

A Look at the News

Television asserts its influence through various tools that convey its messages:

- *Visual interest*   Television needs stories that can be photographed effectively, so it covers fires, crashes, and courthouse scenes.
- *Time*   In 45 seconds or less—a couple of hundred words—television attempts to provide the who, what, when, where, and why of the news.
- *Drama and conflict*   Drama and conflict are two critical elements in a news story and almost always can be found in negative stories, which also are easier to develop and attract larger audiences than positive stories.
- *Ratings*   Interviewers' ratings and reputation are essential to career success. They often have a lot at stake in their relationships with their audiences.

Television news coverage typifies much of how the medium influences all areas of global change. It affects how we live and interact with one another. Television is participant, mirror, and translator of social change and will continue in those roles (see box).

Why Are You There?

You should almost always accept requests for interviews. The empty-chair interview and the behind-these-locked-gates interview are classic examples of what some news-media representatives are tempted to do when one of their invitations to interview is declined.

SOME IMPORTANT POINTS TO KEEP IN MIND

Deadlines are realities.
The reporter wants a good story.
Conflict brings stories to life.
Emphasize communication not confrontation.
Make the interview worthwhile for you.

You should know what you intend to accomplish by being interviewed. Your main purpose is to inform, persuade, solve problems, or help formulate conclusions. In this instant-everything media environment, you must be able to package your messages in a way that appeals to news gatherers and their audiences.

Time Flies

The amount of time you have in which to make your point in any radio or television interview today is brief. News interviews on radio and television used to run as long as 15 minutes, but now it is rare for one to last more than 10 minutes. In fact, more often than not, television news interviews now run only two to four minutes (see box). Other avenues of interviewing can get your point across through the news-reporting media; these opportunities are explored in part 4 of this book.

Not only have the lengths of stories and interviews decreased, but the amount of time interview subjects are allowed to answer a question

---

"A WEEK'S WORTH OF NEWS"

Marjorie Williams, a writer for the *Washington Post Magazine* (May 13, 1990), investigated a "week's worth of news" on a District of Columbia television station. Out of about five hours of "news," Williams computed that the station actually aired "Roughly an hour's worth of commercials, forty minutes of sports, thirty-nine minutes of weather, thirty-six minutes of news relating to Mayor Marion Barry, roughly 20 minutes of self-promotion, including the show's open and close and the 'teases' for stories coming up, and a little more than 14 minutes of national news."

Other than the Barry coverage, the other local news included "nine minutes and 30 seconds on four local murders, five minutes on a Maryland Senate filibuster concerning abortion legislation, five minutes on 'welfare mom' Jacqueline Williams, four minutes of news spread over three days about the Eric Foretich–Elizabeth Morgan custody battle, and two minutes and 40 seconds of foreign news." Of the remaining time, about an hour and five minutes was devoted to miscellaneous news. The longest report all week ran four minutes and 20 seconds; it was a sports segment in which reporter "George Michael rebutted a charge by Howard Cosell that Georgetown University basketball coach John Thompson is racist."

without being interrupted has been curtailed. "Once upon a time," a person being interviewed was allowed at least a minute to respond to a question. In fact, I used to do one-minute drills with clients to show them how much information they could present in a minute on the air. About 10 years ago I noticed that the length of the average response had diminished to about 45 seconds, and in 1988 I realized that the time had been further compressed. Today interviewers are likely to interrupt a guest, or the camera is likely to cut away from the guest and back to the interviewer, once the answer runs 25 seconds.

In today's interview environment, you must be brief. You have to speak in sound bites that are interesting and informative. Your success in doing this will depend on two factors—how well you understand the techniques interviewers use to ask questions and how well prepared you are to respond. Both are covered in chapters 9 and 10.

Preparation Makes the Difference

News interviews enable you to reach audiences that might not have access to or be receptive to your messages in any other ways. When you are properly prepared, they also are more believable than the same information read in a company publication because a third party is generating questions.

Radio and television interviews engage their audiences more than print interviews do, which generally increases memory and retention. Because memory tends to improve when people participate in developing, discussing, or exploring, participants in call-in shows are likely to remember what you say to them. As interviews come to a close, keep in mind that people also remember longest what they hear last.

Interviews also give you an opportunity to make points you have not been able to communicate elsewhere and to clarify points that audiences may have missed or misunderstood.

Interviewers know what interests the public and can help you discover ways to deal with similar issues more effectively in the future. Even hostile questions become opportunities when you are prepared for them. In fact, it is far better for an interviewer to ask such questions than for you to proceed unknowingly when such questions are not asked. Negative questions are best handled with a direct approach.

Consider the media as conduits through which you *reach* audiences—not *as* audiences. Focus on their audiences' agendas. They want to know how your point is relevant to them, so be sure you let them know why they should care.

Some Media Facts

Although reporters look for information and understanding, drama and conflict, brevity and simplicity, they have other needs when they come to you for a story. You are the *source* of the story, or at least one of the sources, so reporters need you and the information you can provide to make a living. Deny them that and they will, indeed, try to get the story elsewhere.

LOW SALARIES

A little-known fact about reporters is their comparatively low salaries. In fact, the *Communicator* (February 1990), a publication of the Radio-Television News Directors Association, reports that in 1989 radio reporters earned an average of $13,000 annually and newscasters-anchors earned $15,600. The highest paid radio newscaster in the nation earned $95,000. Television field reporters earned an average of $18,200, and anchors in the 61 small markets across the country were paid about $28,000. Million-plus salaries were paid only in the three major markets, and only one in 10 network affiliates in the 25 largest markets paid an anchor over half a million dollars a year.

These salary figures mean that in most of your interviews you will be concerned not about the so-called millionaires that are "out to get you" but about the probability that you earn more than the people who ask you questions.

HIGH TURNOVER

Of more concern than salaries is turnover. The March 1990 issue of the *Communicator* indicated that the turnover rate for television news staffs in 1989 was nearly 18 percent and for radio nearly 30 percent. Among news directors—a key position in determining the news that goes on the air—the typical news director had been on the job only about two years, and nearly 25 percent of them had held their post for less than 12 months.

STAFF CUTBACKS

The erosion of news staffs is another factor with which to contend. Television news staffs, already small from previous years' cutbacks, held their own in 1989, but radio news staffs have been eliminated entirely at some stations and reduced from full-time to part-time at others.

In essence, you may find yourself being interviewed by part-time employees who may be relatively new, whose bosses control editorial decisions but may have lived little more than a year in your community, and who may be talking with you about multimillion-dollar concerns while taking home less than 10 dollars an hour. Keep this all in mind as you communicate with reporters and through them with their audiences. Empathy is important in any endeavor. I believe reporters do the best job they can. You have the right to tell your own story in your own way, but if you cooperate with interviewers and attack issues, not people, you are likely to build understanding and acceptance.

How to Make Positive Points

Your primary role in any interview is to respond to questions in ways that make positive points for your organization and help you to win the audience. Gestures and eye contact, preparation and rehearsal, and remaining calm, courteous, and cooperative are important elements to your success that are discussed in later chapters. The following techniques can help you formulate responses that guide the direction of the interview.

FOLLOW-UP QUESTIONS
If you anticipate that you will be participating in a tough interview, keep this in mind: most reporters' follow-up questions are generated by the guest's answers. It should take no more than two or three exchanges before the reporter is guided away from a negative approach and toward constructive questions that stem directly from your positive answers.

Address the issue, and do not attack the interviewer. Interviewers hold the trump cards: they can have the last word or resort to techniques that elicit certain predictable responses. Ignore those techniques, and go directly to the issue. There are no bad questions—only the potential for bad answers for people who have not learned how to score positive points. If you make positive points and follow them with examples, illustrations, quotes, dramatic statistics, or anything else that will make the response interesting, the reporter will have to abandon a negative approach or risk losing the audience's respect by appearing to be a bully.

MILLER'S LAW—"SEVEN PLUS OR MINUS TWO"

According to researcher G. A. Miller, people remember an average of seven bits of information, plus or minus two. This does not mean that you can make up to nine points in an interview. Even the low end of the equation—five points—does not take into account two other factors that occur during interviews: Your five points may follow someone else's seven, which, in turn, are a part of an overall program in which as many as 40 points may be made. The result is overload. I have developed my own rule to cover this: confuse them and you lose them; simplify and you help them buy.

> Confuse them and you lose them.
> Simplify and you help them buy.

During your interviews keep in mind that less is more. Pick two or three points and find as many ways to illustrate them as you can. We all know the KISS formula: Keep It Short and Simple (see box).

"WHAT'D HE SAY?"

Not only does merely 7 percent of your message reach your audience, but audiences tend to forget 40 percent of what they hear after a half hour, 60 percent after a half day, and 90 percent after a week. To increase audience retention involve viewers by addressing issues that concern them and by speaking in a way that captures and holds their interest.

THE POWER OF THREES

Three points are a good number to make during any interview. People accept and recall three topics where just one more creates overload. This example from my book, *Think on Your Feet*, will illustrate:

> Think about such well-known phrases as: "Duty, God, and country," "Faith, hope, and charity," or even, "Up, up, and away!" Now try adding a fourth element to each one. Notice what happens when you say them out loud. Try these: "Duty, God, country, and friends." Or "Faith, hope, charity, and kindness." Or how about, "Up, up, away, and gone!" Clearly, something suffers.

Threes create a definite rhythm, so include your three points in one brief sentence at least once during your interview. When you present information in ways that are familiar to others, they are more likely to pay atention to it, accept it, and recall it.

PREPARING YOUR POSITIVE POINTS

An interview—especially on radio or television—should be approached as conversation and not as confrontation. Reporters usually resort to "devices" only when their guests are unprepared, just plain boring, or defensive in either attitude or responses. Here are some ways to make your points during interviews:

- Anticipate all questions, particularly the antagonistic ones, research the answers, and then practice them *out loud.*
- Make your positive point at the beginning of each answer—*immediately*—and then elaborate.
- Keep your answers brief. The average on-air response to a question on television runs about 45 seconds or less and on radio, about 25 seconds. When you appear on panel programs and talk shows, it is especially important to get right to the point.

YOUR "WORST FEARS" QUESTIONS

After you arm yourself with positive points, develop a list of the questions you are likely to be asked during your interview. Include tough questions that are critical of your position on an issue or the conclusions you have drawn—about anything that is even remotely apt to be asked.

Turn to the list of reporters' techniques in chapter 10 and use it in phrasing your tough questions. Just writing them down in advance helps you remain calm when you encounter them during an interview. In

---

How To Make Positive Points During Interviews

There are several times during an interview when you can assert yourself and make a positive point for your organization. The more obvious ones are when the interviewer

- Asks an easy question
- Pauses more than five seconds
- Compliments you or your organization
- Asks any question that allows you to bridge to your point

PREPARING YOUR POSITIVE POINTS
   Write down the most positive statement you can about

- Your organization
- Its employees
- Its suppliers
- Its method of doing business
- Its customers
- Its profits (or income)
- Its contributions to society
      Financial
      People skills
      Innovations

   Consider competitive wages, good benefits, longevity, continuity of employment, job security, promotion from within, equal opportunity, maintenance programs, safety record, environmental safeguards, ethics, security, testing, monitoring, contributions, scholarships, donated facilities, loaned executives, etc.

   Be brief, but specific. Relate your points to audience interests. Give examples. Show the value to your own organization as well as to others. (This heightens credibility.)

Positive Points to Have Ready for Interviews:

   1. _____
      _____

   2. _____
      _____

   3. _____
      _____

   4. _____
      _____

   5. _____
      _____

PREPARING FOR DIFFICULT QUESTIONS
Write down the most difficult question you could be asked about

- Your organization
- Your issues
- A specific topic
- Your credentials
- Anything else

Write down the one question you hope you will never have to answer about

- Your organization
- Your issues
- The specific topic
- Your credentials or qualifications
- Anything else

rehearsal, follow the format outlined in chapter 5. Ask a helper to aggressively pursue one or two questions if you want to improve your chances for success in the actual situation later. A practice drill will help you realize that none of those ploys can affect you unless you let them. No matter what words questioners use and no matter how they use their voices, you are in charge—of both your attitude and your answers. Keep your own pace, and remain patient and calm. Always try to help achieve understanding: never turn up the heat. If you use each question as an opportunity to show that you are a courteous, cooperative, and calm guest who is willing to share your knowledge of the subject, you can learn to enjoy interviews.

4
Understanding the Interviewer's Personality

K nowing something about interviewers' personalities helps you to be more successful during your interview. Consider entertainment-show hosts David Letterman and Johnny Carson, talk-show hosts Phil Donohue and Oprah Winfrey, anchor personalities Dan Rather and Connie Chung, and morning-show host Bryant Gumbel.

Their faces and voices are known to millions on television, yet they appear on different kinds of programs and each individual has a distinct personality. Observing the styles of people whom you might face on camera helps you anticipate what to expect when you are interviewed.

The Rafe Model—Four-Part Personality Theory

I have developed a tool that is quick and easy to use and that sorts personalities according to criteria that help us communicate more effectively with each type. My model, still in the fine-tuning stages, merges classic approach-avoidance behavioral theory with trait analysis and draws on the work of Raymond B. Cattell, head of the Laboratory for Personality and Group Analysis at the University of Illinois (see box).

This model should be used only for first-time or one-time encounters, since time, additional meetings, or other circumstances may change initial assessments. In simplified form, then, the model categorizes personality traits according to the following behaviors:

CATTELL'S SOURCE TRAITS

    Source trait　1: Reserved—Outgoing
    Source trait　2: Less intelligent—More intelligent
    Source trait　3: Affected by feelings—Emotionally stable
    Source trait　4: Humble—Assertive
    Source trait　5: Sober—Happy-go-lucky
    Source trait　6: Expedient—Conscientious
    Source trait　7: Shy—Venturesome
    Source trait　8: Tough-minded—Tender-minded
    Source trait　9: Trusting—Suspicious
    Source trait 10: Practical—Imaginative
    Source trait 11: Forthright—Shrewd
    Source trait 12: Self-assured—Apprehensive
    Source trait 13: Conservative—Experimenting
    Source trait 14: Group dependent—Self-sufficient
    Source trait 15: Casual—Controlled
    Source trait 16: Relaxed—Tense

Frank J. Bruno, *Behavior and Life: An Introduction to Psychology* (New York: Wiley, 1980).

- Approach (active) people display gregarious actions that show they want to approach *you.*
- Approach (passive) people are reticent yet indicate through their actions that they are willing to have you approach *them.*
- Avoidance (active) people keep you away from them through aggressive behavior.
- Avoidance (passive) people avoid you by withdrawing or acting passively in other ways.

My four-part personality theory considers only those traits having to do with the polarities of approach and avoidance in order to answer the question most important to anyone involved in a communication: Will this person be working with me or against me in this situation? It does not include any of Cattell's trait pairs that do not apply to approach-avoidance categories (such as intelligence) or that apply to either type of personality (such as humility-assertiveness and conservative-experimenting). Some of Cattell's terminology loses its significance when removed from a pair of opposites, so for those terms I developed alternative wording (see box).

APPROACH-AVOIDANCE TRAITS BASED ON CATTELL'S OPPOSING PAIRS

- *Approach traits:* An approach-oriented person may be outgoing, care-free (happy-go-lucky), confident (self-assured), affiliative (group dependent), imaginative, forthright, open-minded (venturesome), relaxed, casual, trusting, conscientious, gentle (tender-minded), and emotional (affected by feelings).
- *Avoidance traits:* An avoidance-oriented person may be tough-minded, shrewd, expedient, analytical or critical (emotionally stable), reserved, sober, practical, controlled, independent (self-sufficient), tense, suspicious, shy, and apprehensive.

Absolutes are rare, and different guests may trigger different behaviors in interviewers, but knowing which behavior best describes the interviewer can help you to become more effective as a guest.

Applying the Model

This model is highly situational, and whether a person is in an approach or an avoidance mode depends on the circumstances, issues or topic, and people involved.

TOOLS USED
Many approach-avoidance signals come through body language, facial expressions, and voice tones, and these nonverbal cues may be in harmony with the questions you are asked or in conflict with them. An interviewer who asks "Well, you've done it this time, haven't you?" may intend any of several meanings, depending on delivery—supportive, sympathetic, snide, or sarcastic. Voice tones, facial expressions, posture, or the way the interview has proceeded are clues to the questioner's intent. It's difficult to say what you may conclude from your observations. Keep in mind, though that your interpretation may be inaccurate. The possibility of misdiagnosis is always present, especially under the stress of an interview.

Here are more of the model's four basic criteria:

- *Approach I (active) ("I want to approach you.")*   These individuals communicate that they want to approach you. They are people-oriented—gregarious, optimistic, enthusiastic, and confident. They have moderated voice tones, their body language is usually open and outreaching, and they maintain friendly but nonaggressive eye contact. Their questions seem to invite you to bring out your best even when the issue is a tough one.

- *Approach II (passive) ("I would accept an approach from you to me.")*   These people are reticent but friendly. They are reserved, but their signals invite approach or dialogue. They are passive, amiable, patient, and self-controlled. They may express a friendly interest in or curiosity about what you have to contribute to the conversation but are less active than approach I people.
- *Avoidance I (active) ("I want to keep you away from me.")*   These people are hostile and aggressive. They want to keep you at a distance from them. They may badger, criticize, and argue and may even try to bully you from time to time. Their voice tones sound pushy and their body language may seem threatening. They are direct, forceful, and impatient.
- *Avoidance II (passive) ("I want to keep me away from you.")*   These people are fearful and insecure. They want to maintain space or distance from others, even if it means withdrawing from you. At times they fall silent, which may cause you to wonder what you should do next, and they appear noncommittal about even your strongest opinions. Their body language tends to be closed, and they may sit with parts of their bodies, such as legs or shoulders, turned slightly away from you. They tend to be analytical, perfectionistic, evasive, and defensive.

Here are some typical postures that signal each type:

- *Approach active*   Relaxed and leaning forward with open posture,
- *Approach passive*   Relaxed and sitting or standing upright with open posture,
- *Avoidance active*   Tense and leaning to one side with closed posture,
- *Avoidance passive*   Tense and leaning slightly back with closed posture.

COMBINING CUES AND TYPES
Most people contain varying elements of the four types of personality traits, but one type generally predominates in any given situation. Deter-

A QUIZ: ANALYZE JOHNNY, OPRAH, AND PHIL

Consider the well-known interviewers who host the various television talk shows and categorize them as approach active, approach passive, avoidance active, or avoidance passive. Then ask another person to analyze the same interviewers. Compare the results. The question to ask is, "What behavior is this person exhibiting?" and not, "How is his or her behavior making me feel?" With practice, you can improve your skills.

Examine the approach-avoidance personalities of local interviewers, as well. Can you identify any local or national interviewers who come on strong or try to trap their guests or pin them against the wall? Do they interrupt guests in midsentence and become argumentative? Does their body language appear confrontational at times, and is it accompanied by aggressive voice tones and words that express strong emotions?

If you have identified an interviewer who displays these signals, you are most assuredly looking at an avoidance I (active) personality.

mining your interviewer's mode during *your* session helps you predict the kinds of responses that probably will be effective.

For the attentive observer, the body provides dozens of messages. The face provides hundreds more clues. Does the interviewer look angry or hostile? Worried or defensive? Bored or dispassionate? Enthusiastic or eager? Active or involved? Supportive or understanding? Calm or complacent? Curious or puzzled? Is his or her head tilted up? Down? Forward? Back? To the side? Held symmetrically and balanced?

Are the interviewer's eyes looking toward you or away? If directly at you, does the intensity indicate a challenge or receptivity? Is the intensity missing, so that they really don't seem to be looking at you at all? Are they looking away? Up? Down? To the side? Are they looking at anything or anyone in particular, or are they again short-focused or gazing into thin air?

Are their mouths relaxed? If so, are they open or closed? Are the lips tense? Are they up, down, straight across, or tilted to one side? Are they curved? Smiling? Frowning?

Consider the other facial muscles. Are they relaxed? Tense? How would you describe what they convey? Acceptance? Boredom? Support? Antagonism? Is the brow furrowed or smooth?

Comparable, shorter checklists can be developed for arms, hands, legs, and feet.

As an experiment, get into this position: lean forward, stare into your imaginary companion's eyes, keep your lips straight across, furrow your brow, tighten your jaw muscles, place your feet flat on the floor, uncross your arms, and clench your hands.

Now imagine a reporter looking at you that way, or ask someone to assume that combination of signals for you. You probably would prefer not to communicate with that reporter.

The Technique in Action

As you observe the interviewer's word choices, voice tones, and non-verbal signals, ask yourself whether you are seeing and hearing approach or avoidance signals. Are they active or passive? Remember that you process these impressions through your personal biases and may misread others' signals or calibrate them incorrectly. You are forming a temporary assessment of the individual's behavior so that you can explore the best possible ways to establish rapport.

WHAT EACH TYPE PREFERS

Most interviewers exhibit both approach passive and avoidance passive behavior. They are not likely to be either gregarious or hostile. Many appear relaxed, in control, and receptive to new information, while at the same time they tend to probe, pressure, and challenge to elicit certain responses with their questions. They also look for proof and assurances.

In general, avoidance passive interviewers like proof, documentation, evidence. They usually welcome a discussion of the pros and cons of any important issue and tend to focus on schedules and plans of action. Provide them with the proof or evidence they need. Be willing to raise the possible objections to your own case; they already may harbor such objections but find themselves reluctant to express these feelings. The key is to offer strong counterarguments to support your case right after you raise each point.

Approach passive interviewers generally let you do most of the work. They tend to leave a lot of silence—gaps that you might be tempted to fill with things you later regret (until you learn how to handle this better; see chapter 10). Your challenge with an approach passive interviewer is to keep them involved. Provide them with specific, low-risk solutions to problems. In preinterview discussions, encourage them to share their views with you and find areas of commonality.

A NOTE OF CAUTION

Some interviewers may shift to avoidance active behavior when they feel your responses are vague, so provide them with documentation and specific outcomes in your answers. Avoid direct disagreement and use logic when you need to persuade. Don't be forceful with your views when they are in this mode.

Some interviewers drift toward approach active occasionally by asking you for testimonials from authorities or recognized experts who support your views. They respond best in this mode when you present information in a friendly and entertaining way and without excessive detail.

When you feel as though you're off to a bad start or that you have a particularly difficult person facing you, try this: postpone judgmental or defensive thinking, keep your own feelings out of the exchange, and work toward better dialogue. Observe the interviewer's behavior merely as a function of the dialogue, and don't get caught up in it. Consider the possibility that others mean to do well by you but may lack the requisite tools for conveying those intentions.

You are always in charge of your own reactions and responses. Nobody can cause you to say things you don't choose to say or feel emotions you choose not to have. In a particularly difficult interview, tell yourself this: no matter what this person may try to do, I will set myself aside from it; I will monitor my behavior carefully and observe theirs, as well.

You believe in your cause and your case. Accept yourself, and make no judgments about this reporter. Assure yourself that he or she is doing what seems right and best. Your patience, tolerance, and understanding will pay dividends during this interview and over the long term, as well.

When you can sustain such feelings, you are less vulnerable to attack and criticism and are better able to empathize with comments such as, "I can understand why you might believe that," or "From your perspective, that might make sense," or "Let's see how we might clarify that."

If you sense that the reporter may be less than objective concerning the issue at hand, watch the intensity of his or her signals. A high intensity of verbal or nonverbal behavior—or conversely, what appears to be overly controlled behavior—may indicate that the reporter has taken a position on the issue. Monitoring approach-avoidance behavior can help you determine this.

If the interviewer appears to have formed a viewpoint that opposes yours before the start the interview, test your observations by asking, "I sense a certain amount of discomfort between us. Is there something I should know before we begin?" Try to determine whether the apparent lack of objectivity has anything to do with the individual's past experience with your organization, you personally, or something else perhaps unrelated to you. Possibly the reporter is having a bad day or is anxious about being unprepared or unable to handle the interview well. Being overly assertive can be a compensation for weaknesses that the interviewer is trying to hide. Clients have reported that interviewers sometimes are initially in awe of them or appear to resent them, perhaps because of their titles, income, or reputations.

In the preinterview chat, do not conclude too early that you know what the other person is thinking or trying to do. These presumptions often prove invalid. Determine whether you can do anything to smoothe the bumps, and then be done with it.

How Far to Go

Just as the interviewer's personality can be defined in approach-avoidance terms, so can the personality of a program, although the host almost always sets the tone. Unless you plan to do a lot of interviewing, however, you may not need this much background information.

A single chapter cannot show you how to do scientifically what you have been doing intuitively throughout a lifetime. However, the study of understanding interviewers' personalities is worth pursuing, and publications on this topic are included in the reading list at the end of this book.

Form versus Substance

Our society often values form over substance and impressions over reality, and the media both reflect and shape this preference. Consider their never-ending scramble for compatibility between television co-anchors as well as between on-camera talent and the people who watch them. The pursuit of ratings and dollars underlies this image making, of course. The point is clear: personality is one of the most important criteria media executives consider in putting news programs and talk shows on the air, particularly in television. Use this fact to gain and use the information that you need to participate in a successful interview.

Part Two
Preparing for the Interview

5
Rehearsing for Interviews

Some people become nervous at the thought of facing an interviewer, and that nervousness escalates when a camera or microphone is involved. Everyone can increase self-confidence through rehearsal, but it has to be the right kind of rehearsal.

Rehearsal Basics

VIDEOTAPE YOUR SESSIONS
If you videotape your practice sessions, you can observe your performance for each interview. Taping frees you from having to remember what you do or say while answering questions in the hope that you will correct it during later rehearsals.

Because content is the least significant element of the audience's reaction to the total interview, your every tone and gesture must be right. Don't memorize your responses to questions you might be asked, but work to understand how interviewers ask questions, how they elicit information from you, how you respond to their techniques, and how you can score positive points.

USE AN ASSOCIATE
To help yourself become comfortable with the process, have an associate ask you questions on camera and keep your initial sessions to about three to five minutes.

START EASY

Your helper should ask only easy questions in the first few sessions so you can practice limiting your answers to about 30 to 45 seconds.

In the next few sessions, have your helper ask the same questions, but phrase them according to some standard interviewers' techniques (see chapter 10). A first-session question such as, "Can you tell me about your excellent employee-benefits program?" might sound like this in later sessions: "You claim to have an excellent employee-benefits program. Is this to counter the criticism that you don't pay very high salaries?"

Playing Hardball

Once you are able to handle questions at this degree of difficulty, you are ready to play hardball. If you don't feel as though you've been through the first two weeks of spring training heavy batting practice after your practice sessions at this level, you probably have not tried hard enough and are not as well prepared as you need to be.

NEGATIVE QUESTIONS

To rehearse at this level, write down every tough question you can think of and phrase them in the meanest, dirtiest, nastiest way imaginable. Make the practice sessions even tougher by throwing in some of the devices interviewers may use to elicit information from you (see chapter 10).

ANTAGONISTIC INTERVIEWERS

When you can handle hardball rehearsals and still feel good about your skills, you are ready for the next level of test. First review your current skills by drilling in this format—planned question one and answer one, planned question two and answer two, and so on. Have your helper take you through a videotaped, five-minute review of easy questions, and critique the tape. Then do a five-minute taping at your second level of questioning, and critique that, as well. If you experienced any difficulties with particular questions at this level, retape a session with your helper asking you only those questions, and play back the segment to see whether you improved. Do this until you have polished your skills to your satisfaction.

Now step back to easier levels to refine another skill—handling follow-up questions. When you answer the first question, your helper should ask you a follow-up that stems logically from your answer. If the first question is something like, "What exactly is your company doing about employee benefits?" you reply by saying, "Well, Jane, our employees tell us they are quite pleased with the benefits package we offer them. They can use our new menu-options approach to add benefits of their own choosing to our basic plan. The menu approach serves their specific needs and helps keep the costs of our programs down, as well." Now the hard-ball follow-up to this response takes a negative turn. Jane gets tough and comes back with something such as this: "Aren't you really saying that your company is too cheap to give its employees all the coverage they might need? Isn't this a cop-out? Do a five-minute session at this level, critique the tape, and then go back and polish your answers to any questions that gave you particular difficulty.

Finally, you are ready for the additional twist. No matter how you answer a question, your helper will attack you with difficult questions and follow-ups, and antagonistic and argumentative delivery. She should interrupt you, criticize you personally, question your ethics, and so on—far more aggressively than any self-respecting actual interviewer would do. The rehearsal may seem unrealistic, but it prepares you for whatever interview situations you might encounter in the future.

Critiquing the Tapes

In your rehearsals you have been working on the content of your responses, but your voice tones and other nonverbals account for 83 percent of your communication. Use the rehearsal evaluation checklist to help you assess your performance (see box).

COMMON PROBLEMS
Replay all the tapes, noting what you do well—what communicates the right impressions to your audience—and what you need to improve or eliminate. Particularly note eye contact, facial expressions, posture, and vocal and physical nervous habits or mannerisms you should control.

As you observe from a viewer's perspective, not from your own or your organization's, ask yourself, "What do I think about the person I'm watching on this TV?" Be as objective as you can, and you will have a good idea about how others will respond to your performance. Using the

REHEARSAL EVALUATION CHECKLIST

This checklist can help you and an associate critique each of your interviews and record your progress. You are invited to reproduce it only for your own use and no other.

Put an asterisk (*) beside each point you handle well and an X beside each point you need to work on further. You do not have to put a mark beside each category.

Date _____ Difficulty level _____

Nature of rehearsal _____

Content _____

Attribute	Score	Comments
Overall attitude	_____	_____
Gestures	_____	_____
Facial expression	_____	_____
Eye contact	_____	_____
Posture	_____	_____
Poise	_____	_____
Movement	_____	_____
Voice level	_____	_____
Voice tones	_____	_____
Pacing	_____	_____
Modulation	_____	_____
Enunciation	_____	_____
Convictions	_____	_____
Handling of questions	_____	_____
Handling of questioner	_____	_____
Scoring positive points	_____	_____
Registering "sparklers"	_____	_____

four-part personality model discussed in chapter 4 as your guide, determine whether your voice, nonverbals, and words convey a balance between Approach I (active or approach*ing*) and Approach II (passive or approach*able*). If they do, a few easy interviews followed by series of increasingly difficult ones will help you become a skilled spokesperson.

If you ask others their opinion of the tape, do not seek critiques from people who know you well or who are in competition with you professionally or socially. Seek the advice of people whose opinions of others have been shown to be accurate in key situations in the past.

INTERRELATED PROBLEMS

Sometimes interview problems are interrelated. Your body language—particularly your facial expressions—may reveal any difficulty you have in answering basic tough questions. Your voice tones may convey any annoyance you feel with yourself. The audience, unfortunately, cannot distinguish between your momentary annoyance with your own interview skills and a lapse of patience with the interviewer. At best, the audience hears annoyed or frustrated voice tones, sees a face that reflects the same emotions, and listens to an answer whose content may not reflect what you wanted to say. Rather than empathize with you or pity you, they may simply turn you off—literally as well as figuratively. You will have failed to deliver your message.

Coaching   Coaching someone to overcome these problems requires a detailed analysis of the individual, the problem, the possible causes or triggers of undesirable behaviors, and the nature of the behavioral changes that need to be made. You can do some self-coaching by finding a place in your early rehearsals where you were doing well, locating a subsequent ineffective response, analyzing what changed, considering how it changed, and assessing whether the problem grew slowly or came on abruptly. You can correct a gradual deterioration by rehearsing more at the levels at which you attained 100 percent success. A problem that comes on abruptly, however, usually is corrected only with discussion about the emotions that you experienced during your response—what "hot buttons" may have been touched and so on. You can considerably reduce emotional responses by constantly monitoring your own attitudes and actions and by focusing on collaborating with—not confronting—your interviewer.

Expanding Your Gestures   During difficult rehearsals, gestures tend to diminish considerably. People withdraw within themselves under pressure, almost as though making themselves smaller targets was a fundamental survival behavior. If your gestures become virtually nonexistent, your positive voice tones and general enthusiasm also may suffer.

Because gestures are one of the most important tools you can use during a news-media interview—particularly one that is televised—you need to ensure that your gestures are sufficiently expansive.

Videotape another five-minute rehearsal, and gesture as expansively as you can during each response. By gesturing to the extreme, you will be better prepared to moderate to a more acceptable level in later rehearsals. This is an excellent warm-up technique to practice before actual interviews.

When you watch the replay of this exercise, you probably will notice that your gestures do not look as overdone in the playback as they may have felt when you were taping. Television absorbs large quantities of vocal and physical energy.

Before each rehearsal, do the exercises described in chapter 7, in sequence, selecting the ones that are best for you. The repeated association between warm-up exercises and successful rehearsals carries over to actual interviews and helps you refine your responses.

6
Preparing Yourself Physically

Your general appearance is important to the overall message you convey in television interviews. The following tips about clothing, makeup, general grooming, microphones, health, voice, and travel should help you physically prepare for your performance.

Clothing

Keep your clothing simple, tasteful, and appropriate. Don't wear very new or very old clothes. Dress appropriately for your occupation and position and according to others' expectations of how you should look. When local customs and conventions dictate shirts instead of jackets or slacks instead of skirts, dress more formally. Slacks are rarely appropriate interview attire for women. Both men and women should avoid shorts (bare legs) and short sleeves (bare arms) on television unless they have a very good reason for dressing that way.

Women can wear suits, dresses, coordinates, skirts and blazers or tasteful skirts and blouses. The style should be appropriate to the time the interview will be aired—morning, afternoon, or evening. As a general rule, understated is better than overdone.

Men should wear suits, although conservative blazers are appropriate in some situations. Avoid vests. They encase the body, cut off circulation, entrap body heat, and tend to add the appearance of weight when worn on camera.

COLORS AND PATTERNS

If you wear a suit, a muted pinstripe is acceptable, with a small, thin stripe preferable to a wide stripe. Patterns and checks can cause a distracting, wavy, or vibrating image on the home screen when the clothing pattern crosses with the dot-matrix pattern of the screen. (To see approximately what this looks like, lay one piece of window screening over another at various angles and look through them into the light.)

Executives should not wear brown suits. Surveys show that the public identifies brown suits with the working class. For your interviews, consider gray or blue—lighter shades in warm weather, darker shades in cold weather. Have all buttons in place and secured tightly.

COMFORT LEVELS

Wear lightweight clothing, even in winter. Never wear winter-weight clothing for television studio interviews. Some studios have hot lights, and heavy clothing tends to cause people to perspire.

Tight clothing tends to call attention to extra pounds. Loose clothing tends to hide those pounds and is more comfortable. Try not to wear a collar so loose that it makes your neck look skinny, however. Dark colors tend to diminish body size, and light colors tend to increase it.

ON THE ROAD

If you are traveling or may have interviews in your office unexpectedly, have a fresh shirt or blouse handy at all times. Remember to rotate it through your laundry occasionally. One plant manager told me about the time reporters arrived at the receptionist's office unexpectedly. He reached behind his closet door for his "spare" shirt, opened the plastic travel bag, and discovered that a mouse had taken up residence and left a nest, along with a few other goodies, in the shirt pocket.

If you are likely to wrinkle or rumple your clothing before an interview, you should either change to another outfit or touch up whatever your wearing. A portable steamer helps. When you look your best before an interview, you will feel better about the process that is about to take place.

IMPORTANT TIPS ON LIGHTING

Television cameras read for light levels, so the camera lens adjusts to the lightest or darkest colors it sees. This affects how you look on camera. For example, in a medium shot in which the color of your dark attire dominates, the camera's iris adjusts to the dark colors that predominate and your skin, if light, may appear washed out. If the camera takes a medium shot in which your very light clothing predominates, the camera's iris closes up to reduce the amount of light coming in, and if you have a dark complexion, your facial features could be lost.

The simplest way to handle this lighting problem is to balance your skin tones with the colors you wear on camera. This is useful when you are having still photographs taken for newspapers and magazines, as well. One of the most difficult photographs I was ever asked to take early in my career was of a black man who was very dark complected, wearing a light-colored suit, standing in front of a dark background with two light-complected white men who were also wearing light suits. It was necessary to provide supplemental lighting for the black man's face and to separate his face from the dark background, but without washing out all three men's suits and the two white men's faces.

NECKWEAR

Women's ties, scarves, and shawls can be blue, grey, burgundy, or other colors that do not call attention to themselves. Men's ties should be plain with basic, solid colors or large patterns, which tend not to appear to vibrate on television. Adjust your tie or scarf properly *before* you face an interview. Men should tie their neckties a bit shorter for seated television appearances. Otherwise, when they sit down, the ties will drape in their laps and make them look unkempt.

SHOES

Shoes should be conservative and reflect good taste. For men, dress slip-ons, lace-ups, or wing-tips are most appropriate. Women should avoid open-toe shoes and overly high heels because they are seen as impractical, especially in rain, snow, or cold weather. Both men and women should make certain the heels and soles of their shoes are not worn down and that the shoes are well polished.

Men should wear black shoes with blue or grey suits. Women who wear blue or grey outfits can wear black shoes or coordinate with blue, grey, or burgundy—lighter shades in warm weather.

GENERAL APPEARANCE

In a standing interview, button your jacket if you're wearing one. In a seated interview, unbutton the jacket, but pull it together at the middle. Especially in the seated interview, straighten your jacket behind you so that it does not bunch up.

You want nothing to divert attention from your professionalism and your message, but short skirts and trousers are likely to do that. Men should wear trousers long enough to break slightly at the crease and yet not ride up when men sit. Men's socks must be high enough to keep bare legs from being exposed when the wearer sits with his legs crossed.

Because television camera angles sometimes are low, women should wear skirts that extend about an inch below the knee when the wearer is sitting. At least two morning shows I have watched try to hide their female anchor's short skirts by placing a pot of flowers strategically on a coffee table, which only further identifies the short skirt as a problem. Women should carry extra stockings to avoid appearing on camera with a run.

Jewelry and other accessories should be kept to a minimum. Wear nothing that may jangle, flash, or otherwise distract the viewer or call attention to itself.

Carry nothing in your pockets. Empty your pockets before you go on camera. Bulges are not attractive, and in a standing interview, people under stress tend to fidget with items in their pockets. Your accessories should be of top quality. Never carry pens in an outside pocket, and especially avoid plastic pocket liners for pens.

Makeup

Try to schedule appearances in the morning—before new beard growth emerges or makeup begins to fade. For interviews occurring after midday, men should shave again (with an electric shaver to avoid nicks and cuts) and women should reapply makeup.

Before putting on makeup for the interview, men should apply aftershave, and women should use an astringent, to close up facial pores.

Ask the person who books your interview whether makeup will be available to you. Generally it is. Allow yourself to be made up at the studio. If you plan to interview on television or appear on camera frequently and anticipate finding yourself in situations where makeup is not available, however, speak with someone who knows about television makeup and then purchase the simplest kit of materials you need. Someone who knows how to select makeup for television and can teach you to apply it can give you sound advice about how to counter the special problems posed by the source, location, and intensity of television lighting.

If you are a man, expect not to like what you see when you are made up the first time. Keep in mind that your purpose is to restore a natural balance to compensate for the strong lighting of television, the technicalities of cameras and equipment, and the distortions of two-dimensional televised images.

Women who have the option of removing street makeup and having the studio do their makeup should do so. If you do your own makeup before you go to the television studio, however, there are some rules to follow (rules that apply to men, as well). Keep your makeup soft and natural. Avoid evening makeup. Avoid frosted makeup: it makes faces look bloated. Be sure it is well blended with no obvious lines of demarcation. Go light on what you apply. One of the top cosmetologists in television once told me that a woman's biggest grooming mistake is to overdo her makeup. "Don't come in looking like Tammy Fay Bakker," she cautions, "unless you have a very good reason."

Your foundation should be the same shade as your skin tone or one shade darker. You should also cover your entire face and neck with a sheer foundation, blending in a slightly darker shade over just your face before applying blush and eye makeup. Consider using a foundation to cover your hands or bald spots. Apply liquid or cake makeup on your head with sponges for a matte or natural look.

If your skin is light then you should use complimentary eyeliner. Do not use black or dark brown eyeliner. Whatever shade is used, it should be applied with a soft edge, not a harsh line.

Avoid blues and strong reds. The cameras tend to overemphasize them. Women should avoid dark lipstick and use natural shades instead. Men generally do not have lipgloss applied unless their lips are overly red, and then a base color may be used to tone them down.

On camera, the eyes are extremely important. Your eyebrows should either match or appear slightly lighter than your hair color. If you use eye shadow, earth and natural tones are generally best for most studio lighting conditions. Concentrate on the outer corners to make your eyes look larger. Men especially need to ensure that makeup is not obvious on camera.

If you use a blush, apply it to your cheekbones rather than to the center of your cheeks. Blend it out to your ears and feather it lightly at the edges; otherwise, the resultant line will make your ears appear to stick out.

Since your purpose in wearing makeup is to prevent reflected light from making you look washed out, your last step in applying makeup is to dull any part of your skin that is exposed to the camera. This helps absorb the studio's strong lighting and enables you to look more natural.

To eliminate shine and to set your makeup, powder should be applied after foundation and before blush or eye makeup. If you need to be repowdered ("dusted") between takes or during commercial breaks, blot your face with a tissue first to remove perspiration. This keeps the new powder from caking. Corn Silk™ translucent pressed powder is extremely effective, although any pressed or loose translucent (noncolored or faint flesh-toned) powder works.

The overhead lighting in studios tends to accentuate deep-set eyes as well as lines, scars, bags, dark shadows, large pores, and blemishes. Any highlighter that is lighter than your skin color may be useful in covering these since highlighters reflect light and tend to diminish flaws. Highlighters should be applied before foundation. If the problems are still evident, use more highlighter over the foundation and then apply powder.

Other Grooming Tips

NAILS
Men and women should make sure their nails are neatly manicured and check to see that their hair is neatly combed or brushed.

HAIR
Women can have their hair done before an interview but should not experiment with a new hairdo. Long hair should be kept from falling into the face. Men should not get a new haircut within three days of an appearance. Although you should not appear on television needing a haircut, a fresh haircut can make you look scalped. Close haircuts also tend to convey the impression that the individual saves pennies by having enough cut off to prolong the grow-out time.

EYEGLASSES
If you wear eyeglasses, avoid metal rims, which tend to flare on camera. If you have no alternate frames that you can wear for an interview, and if your hair is long enough to cover the earpieces, tip them up slightly to direct the light's reflection away from the camera. You also can spray your frames (not the lenses) with the dulling spray that is used to cover the gloss on photographs. Do not wear photosensitive glasses on cam-

era. They darken and convey a secretive impression. For the same reason, do not wear sunglasses, either. The audience needs to see your eyes to complete the communication: don't hide them.

Microphones

The crew probably will put on your microphone for you. It is generally a clip-on mike that is hardwired into the sound system. Be sure the clothing you wear enables the mike to be put on easily. "Dressing the mike" can be tricky with a shawl neck sweater.

If no one offers to help you put it on, clip the microphone about a handspan beneath your chin or near the third button on a man's dress shirt. Don't allow it to touch any loose part of your clothing. If the interviewer is seated beside you, clip it to the side to which your head will be turned most of the time. Otherwise it doesn't matter. Think of the device as a tie clip with an ornament (the mike head) on it; the mike head faces outward where it can pick up your voice.

Tuck the excess wire from your microphone as far out of sight as possible for appearance's sake and so you do not hook the cord with your hands and detach the mike when gesturing. Generally, I run the wire down behind my necktie, secure it in place by opening a shirt button, buttoning it back over the wire, tucking the cord just under the waistband of my trousers, and running it around to my side, where I let it drop under my jacket behind the chair.

Health

HOW AND WHAT TO EAT
Eat properly before an interview or appearance. Your body must have the right kind of nourishment if it is to put forth its best effort. Avoid carbohydrates or heavy, starchy foods; they can induce fatigue. Also avoid any foods with excess roughage such as natural cereals, whole-grain muffins, nuts, and berries; they can lodge in your throat and impede the interview process.

Do not drink hot or chilled beverages just before you go on. Cold constricts the vocal cords, and heat expands them: either one can cause problems with your voice. For similar reasons, avoid milk and cheese products, which tend to thicken mucus in the throat. Relax your throat by sipping a moderately warm glass of water just before you go on. Some people prefer weak tea with honey and lemon, black coffee, or a slightly flat cola product that is warmed to room temperature. Sip slowly.

Avoid alcohol-based products. They do not help and can give you a false sense of confidence while interfering with your response rate.

THE IMPORTANCE OF REST

If you know at least a day ahead of time that you have an interview scheduled, get a good night's sleep. Even an hour's rest before you are interviewed is better than going on camera feeling fatigued. It helps you concentrate and focus clearly on your message.

Should you have difficulty falling asleep, drink a glass of warm milk. Warming it releases chemicals that can help the brain relax. You also can try light stretching exercises and a hot shower just before going to bed.

As you begin to fall asleep, make certain your thoughts are positive. Here is a message many of my clients have found helpful—one I have used myself: "I have done my best. I have prepared myself for tomorrow. Now I'm feeling very relaxed. My eyes are growing heavy. I can feel my head, my arms, my legs, and all of my body slowly easing, relaxing deeper and deeper into the bed as I let go and enjoy a comfortable, restful sleep." As you say this, allow your words to match your breathing rate, slowing down more and more with each affirmation.

You also can try relaxing each part of your body progressively. Tense your toes, then allow them to relax as you tell yourself that your toes are now relaxed. Work your way up your body progressively. When you reach your stomach, shift out to your fingers and work your way back in until you reach your stomach again. Now concentrate on the muscles in your buttocks, then on the small of your back, gradually working up your spine. When you reach your shoulders, shift your emphasis to the top of your head and work your way down through all your facial muscles (eyes, ears, nose, mouth, and jaw). Move to your neck and follow the same procedure.

If you still have not managed to fall asleep, tense every single muscle in your body at once, then let go. As you release, picture anything you find tranquil and peaceful. Hold that image and tell yourself that you are sinking warmly, deeply, and pleasantly into total relaxation.

Your Voice

Since radio and television audiences form 38 percent of their total impression of your message from *how* you speak, developing a good speaking voice is important. It is not necessary to sound like the people who interview you, but you should care for your voice and use it properly.

THROAT CONDITIONS

To take care of your voice, have a good attitude toward the stressful events in your life and pay attention to how your voice responds to those events. Listen for the early signs of fatigue, stress, allergy, or a cold. If you have frequent colds, allergies, or sinus problems and feel that over-the-counter remedies are not helpful, see your doctor.

If you plan to do a lot of interviewing, avoid chills, dampness, drafts, and sudden changes in temperature. Stay out of drying winds, and avoid smoke and fumes.

Immediately before an interview, try not to cough: it can irritate the lining of the throat and make your speaking voice sound raspy. If you have a cold or need to clear your throat, try sipping a glass of warm water for about five minutes before you go on. If you feel you need a cough drop, use one that has a glycerine base, but be sure you have nothing in your mouth during the interview.

If you need to reduce the symptoms of a cold, allergy, hayfever, or sinus condition, avoid medications that contain antihistamines unless they are absolutely essential. Substitute a product that will help keep your throat moist. As a last resort, you might try a product such as Glyoxide®, which has a glycerine base and is used in dental hygiene. Place a few drops on the back of your tongue before your interview and allow the liquid to ease down your throat and coat it. This also helps overcome the initial dry-throat syndrome that can occur under the stress of interviewing.

If you have a bad cold and must go on the air, saturate a face towel with water as hot as you can tolerate, then place it over your face and gently inhale the steam. You might also try inhaling anything with menthol in it that is otherwise harmless. One workshop participant puts a menthol cough drop in a cup of boiling water and then inhales the vapors.

If you have a cold and must be out in cold weather before an interview—say, in a crisis situation—keep a scarf, handkerchief, or even the turned-up collar on your jacket or coat over your mouth and breathe into that until you go on camera. This should give you temporary relief.

During an interview, you can add moisture to a dry throat without calling attention to yourself by nipping the tip of your tongue between your teeth. You can make this work even better if you think of squeezing a lemon and sucking in the juice as it drips. Try this trick right now. It does work.

If your diet lacks the consistency and nutrition you need to maintain good health, especially if you have to go on the road for a series of interviews, consider using a vitamin supplement.

To ease tension in your throat, jaw, and facial muscles, be sure to get proper rest and speak in a range that is comfortable for you. This may help.

None of these suggestions should be considered a substitute for a visit with your doctor—particularly if you suffer from chronic tension or raspiness, or other recurring problems such as snapping or popping in your jaw area. In such cases, seek the guidance of a knowledgeable professional.

WHAT YOUR VOICE CAN ACCOMPLISH

Your voice can help you communicate in many ways. How you use its range, volume, pace, intensity, inflection, and even pauses can have a major effect on your messages. The way you articulate is also important, as is what I call static.

Range   When you are interviewed, speak within your normal range. Do not create vocal strain by trying to pitch your voice lower than it really is in the belief that this will make you sound more authoritative. You could end up with vocal strain and raspiness and sound even less commanding.

Volume   Your speaking volume should be comfortable for you and appropriate to the circumstances. If you learn to project properly, you will not have to yell to be heard—even under the most difficult of circumstances. One of the most common mistakes people make is to yell into a microphone when there is a lot of noise around them, forgetting that the sound engineer can simply boost the microphone's gain control if you speak in a normal voice.

Pace   The pace or rate at which you speak is also important. A normal pace is about 150 words per minute. Rapid is about 200 words per minute, and slow is anything below 100 words per minute. Your pace is affected by regional influences, stress or relaxation, and even whether you tend to be a visual person (rapid speech) or a tactile or kinesthetic one (slow speech).

If your accent may be unfamiliar to your particular audience and you tend to speak at a moderate to rapid pace, begin your responses to questions at a slow, even pace. This gives listeners a chance to tune in to the way you pronounce your words. Ideally, you should level off to at about 150 words per minute. To check this, record yourself on tape when you are not being interviewed and listen to your natural pace. For variety and dramatic impact, from time to time you can speak more rapidly, more slowly, or even in a staccato fashion in which you emphasize each individual word.

Intensity   Your intensity is reflected in vocal tension and the emphasis you place on words. Depending on how you say it, "Now that's hot" can mean that something finally heated up, that this particular item is hot, or that the heat is particularly intense.

Inflection   If you add inflection or emphasis, you can also convey anger, a note of caution, surprise, satisfaction, and much more.

Pauses   Pauses are yet another tool. During an interview, pauses give you a second or two to collect your thoughts or to allow your silence to underscore a point you have just made. As long as you use pauses only once or twice in an interview that runs five minutes or longer, they can add another useful dimension to your overall message.

Articulation   Your ability to articulate, or to pronounce words properly and enunciate clearly, is also important. If audiences focus on how you say words or run words together, your meaning may slip right by them. For help with standard pronunciations, listen carefully to national radio and television newscasters or use the pronunciation guide found in your dictionary.

Static   Finally, consider eliminating static when you speak. Static includes phrases that do not not contribute to good speech, such as "it's like," "you know," and "okay." It also includes filler sounds such as "uh" or "and" and even "and, uh."

Although everyone occasionally use such words and sounds—particularly when they are tired, unprepared, or anxious—they add nothing to a successful interview. If you feel yourself about to use a static word, say nothing and force yourself to say a real word instead.

Your voice is an important tool. Never underestimate its power in any communication. It accounts for 38 percent of the total message your audience receives.

Travel without Stress

If you plan to tour several states and participate in interviews with various stations and publications, you should find some of these tips helpful—even if you plan no more than one trip this year.

AIRLINE TICKETS
Order your travel tickets well before your trip and ask a lot of questions—especially about scheduling. Sometimes you can avoid changing planes or having your luggage make a separate trip by scheduling a flight just minutes before or after the one you originally considered.

Know where your connecting flights depart from. In some airports, you should allow at least a half hour between connections or you may need jogging shoes.

When you order your tickets, ask whether a meal will be served, and, if so, request a special meal. Most airlines offer low-fat, low-cholesterol, low-salt, kosher, and other meal alternatives. Any option must be

---

To practice the skills just discussed, read the following sentence in every way possible, varying one of your vocal tools each time: "What an interview this one is going to be."

How you say these words can change their meaning in several ways. Be sure you say it the way you mean it, and mean it when you say it. To illustrate the point, think about how you might deliver this line: "I can't recommend news-media interviews too highly."

prepared individually and usually tastes better than the prepackaged fare other passengers receive. You also may want to carry a protein snack, such as peanuts or cheese.

Once in the air, drink water. Plane cabins are notoriously lacking in humidity, and your throat will benefit from the extra moisture. Use chewing gum if cabin pressure causes ear problems for you.

If you travel coach, request an aisle seat when you order your tickets, unless you intend to sleep through the entire flight. Aisle seats provide more shoulder room, leg room, and freedom to stretch your legs. Avoid the bulkhead seats—the ones that have the cabins' divider wall in front of you. They provide no room for underseat storage, and most airlines put passengers with babies in those seats. Try not to sit in the row behind the bulkhead seats. Babies like to stand up, lean over the back of the seat, and bomb you with anything from cookies to bottles.

After you order your tickets, either pick them up yourself or have them hand delivered to you. Check them against your itinerary. Mistakes happen.

PACKING

Write your list of what you think you will need, and then strip it down to the minimum. Your goal should be to carry everything you need directly onto the plane. Luggage-handling stories aside, carry-on luggage saves you from walking to a distant luggage area and waiting to retrieve your belongings before you can get underway. Travel with one overhead bag and one underseat bag. Avoid a briefcase unless you really need it. In the side pouch of your carry-on, keep handy everything that you will need on the flight, including whatever book you happen to be reading.

CLOTHING

For two to five overnights, I generally pack two suits, two neckties, and a daily change of shirt, underwear, and socks (plus an extra pair of socks in case of wet feet). Women can generally follow the same rule, substituting as appropriate.

On the road, you can wear three-season clothing, such as a tropical wool, year-round. You rarely will be outdoors long enough to need heavy wool. Top quality wool blends shed wrinkles best.

A trench coat with a zip-out lining, a wool scarf, and a pair of gloves are sufficient outerwear for all except extremely cold and windy cities in the winter. In those cities I carry a full-length, down-filled coat that compresses into a very small bundle and earmuffs or a pullover hat that tucks into a pocket.

Unless you will be on the road three or more days, you probably will not use the hotel's sauna, pool, or exercise room so don't bother to pack a swimsuit, robe, sweats, or athletic shoes. On longer trips, carry a set of casual clothes for brief ventures to whatever attractions the city may offer.

TOILETRIES

Regular-sized containers of shampoo, hairspray, and so on take up too much room and add too much weight. Transfer what you need into small plastic containers that have reliable seals (I buy mine in a camping-supplies store), put these into a sealable plastic bag, and for good measure put the bag into a leak-proof kit made for personal items. Carry small containers for your shaving cream, toothpaste, deodorant, and other items, too.

Hotel Check In   When you check into your hotel, leave a wake-up call. When you arrive at your room, place a call for messages. Don't ask for them at the front desk: calling alerts the operator that you are now registered and also identifies your correct room number for him or her. Leave another wake-up call, and set your alarm to go off five minutes later than whatever time you have asked to be called.

Never leave valuables in your room. In fact, think twice about wearing valuable jewelry. Cleaning personnel often leave open several hotel room doors at a time, and whenever I have taken something from my room while a maid was cleaning, I have never been challenged. If you must leave items of value in your room, store them in soiled laundry items in a plastic bag inside your carry-on luggage.

JET LAG

I have no solution to the problem of jet lag: sometimes I feel energized after a trip, sometimes I feel exhausted, and sometimes I feel no effects of the trip at all. Listen to what your mind and body are telling you, and do whatever you feel will help you best. Scientists at Harvard University, Massachusetts General Hospital, and Tufts University have treated severe cases of jet lag with a hormone called melatonin, which is produced in the brain's pineal gland. Apparently it has no side effects. Speak with your doctor about melatonin if jet lag is a problem for you.

7
Preparing to Appear

P hysical and emotional comfort contribute to any successful experience, and attitude is extremely important in media appearances and interviews. The fear of speaking before an audience has been called this country's number-one fear: adding cameras and microphones intensifies this fear.

The Body Mirrors the Mind

When we experience nervousness or apprehension, the body adapts its functions accordingly. Muscles tense, heartbeat quickens, blood surges, faces flush, and so on. You may notice lightheadedness, a pulsing in your head, or ringing sounds in your ears. Involuntary and voluntary organs and muscles are activated: you may have difficulty breathing, perspire, feel a chill, feel your throat is dry, or feel a trembling in your jaw or other parts of your body. You may even feel disconnected from your body or want to flee as quickly as possible.

In a new or unfamiliar situation—such as when you face interviewers, cameras, and microphones—the physiological stimulation may be particularly strong. Your mind's appraisal of the situation triggers hormones and glandular responses that prepare you for the fight or flight response: in other words, you are scared.

These emotions enable us to protect ourselves from anything that might threaten, or appear to threaten, it. The key to managing this natural drive toward self-preservation lies in our ability to change our

61

mind's perceptions of what is threatening to us and what is not. Centuries ago, the Greek philosopher, Epictetus, noted that it is not events that trouble us but rather our perception of those events.

Preventing unwanted symptoms is a relatively simple process, thanks to a few tools available to us from the behavioral sciences and the mind's ability to think rationally. In most cases in life, our worst fears never materialize, and when they do, they are of less consequence than we anticipated. Franklin Delano Roosevelt was right when he said, "The only thing we have to fear is fear itself." The trauma you might anticipate after you accept an interview may never happen in the actual situation, especially if you follow the guidance offered in this book.

Change the State

If you find yourself becoming stressful and nervous, do the opposite of what your mind is causing you to do. For example, if your breathing is short, breathe more deeply. If you are tensing your muscles, loosen them. If you are sitting in a way that conveys apprehension, sit more confidently.

Your body and mind are linked, and therefore your thoughts and your actions are, too. Research has shown that when we change our postures and actions to those that correspond with the emotions we would like to experience, the mind follows. Changes in our physiological state produce corresponding changes in our emotions. The physical act triggers neurochemical processes in the brain where the mind's perception of what it is "supposed to" feel is then altered. To put it simply, if you don't like your feelings, change them.

What Emotions Look Like

Think about what a calm and confident person looks like, and assume that posture when you are least likely to think about it—just as you are about to feel nervous or stressful. The quickest way to communicate the perception of power in a media interview or appearance is to make certain your nonverbal messages convey confidence. As long as your message is consistent with the emotions you are trying to convey, if you act confident, you will feel confident, and people will perceive you as being confident.

Practice in situations that you perceive as being of low threat, and each success will build your skill to higher levels. The next time you feel nervous, hold your head high, stand erect, square your shoulders, and begin breathing slowly, deeply, and rhythmically. No matter what your thoughts might be at the moment, continue in this manner. You soon should begin thinking more positively about the situation.

Change Your Body, Change Your Emotions

Interviews can be stressful, and people under stress tend to concentrate their tensions in one body area—across the forehead, behind the eyes, in the temples, throat, jaws, neck, shoulders, chest, stomach, or various joints.

Avoid chemicals that purportedly help you relax before interviews and speaking engagements. None will give you what you need, especially over the long run. You are better off to recognize your stress, deal with it, and then get on with doing your job. Skilled athletes never enter a competition without loosening up and getting their mental processes aligned toward the event. Skilled spokespersons know that facing interviewers demands the same effort.

LOOSENING UP
When you feel stress before an interview, you may worry that the interviewer or the home audience will notice it. If you allow the stress to prevail and try to control it, you may cause even more tension. Doing exercises that can help you have a better interview is like exercising for any other purpose.

The exercises here are especially useful to anyone who needs to face television cameras. Keep your own physical considerations in mind, and feel free to use other exercises that relieve stress and help you increase your positive energy levels. Consult with your doctor before you begin.

Warm Hands   Before your interview, concentrate on where the tension is physically located, shake your hands loosely and rapidly, rag-doll fashion, clap them together, or swing them out to your sides and across your chest allowing your open palms to slap your upper arms lightly. This stimulates circulation and warms your hands. Immediately put your hands on the stressful area and concentrate on "bringing warmth" through your hands to relieve the stress. Doing this helps to burn off the stress and also takes your mind off your emotions. It is a form of displacement, or substitute, behavior—a way to busy the body, burn off the physical manifestations of stress, and free your mind to focus on more useful activities.

Lie Down   Lie down, elevate your feet, and take the pressure off your spine, neck, and shoulders. This helps circulate oxygen through the blood stream and into the brain, which, in turn, helps encourage clearer thinking and lower stress levels.

Sky Hook   For neck and jaw tension use your neck muscles to raise your head higher above your shoulders. Imagine that someone is cradling your head gently and is lifting it lightly toward the ceiling. Allow yourself to experience a floating feeling.

Coat Hanger   Now lift your shoulders toward your ears. Imagine a coat hanger through your sleeves and you and your coat hanging up in a closet so that your feet barely touch the ground. As you assume this position, take a deep breath, and feel the light, comfortable stretching that occurs. Hold this posture for two counts, and then let your shoulders drop like a wet washcloth. Do this 10 times. If you feel like yawning at any time during these exercises, do so.

Giraffe   Next, stretch your neck out, gently and slowly, and start curving your back over so that you face the floor. Picture a giraffe easing down as you do this. Allow your head to lower slowly about 6 to 12 inches. Do this 10 times.

Swivel   Now, do the giraffe one more time, but when your head is as far as you can extend it comfortably, look up slowly toward your left ear. Allow gravity to bring it back to the center, then look up slowly toward your right ear. Allow it to drop to the center again, and return to your upright position. Do this 10 times.

Circles   Next, extend your elbows out to your sides and fold your hands in toward your chest. Allow your fingers to touch lightly. Using only your shoulders, trace circles in the air with your elbows. Do this forward 10 times. Lower your arms for four counts, then resume the elbows-out position again. Now trace the circles to the rear 10 times. Lower your arms.

Racing Diver   Now face the palms of your hands in toward your sides and bring your arms behind you as racing swimmers do before they dive into the pool. Your thumbs are pointing down. Gradually rotate them up toward your body, as high as you can. Hold for two counts, then rotate them as far as you comfortably can in the opposite direction. Hold for two counts, then allow your arms to return to your sides. Do this 10 times.

Tripod   Next, spread your feet to a comfortably wide stance, like two legs on a sturdy tripod. Shift most of your weight to your right side and lower your body to where you can feel a gentle tug running down behind your *left* leg. Rise up and down enough to feel this light tug 10 times. Return to an upright position for four counts. Now repeat the procedure on the opposite side.

Fruit Picker   Reach both hands high over your head and imagine yourself plucking two large grapefruit out of a tree. Stretch your fingers widely as though to grasp the fruit, then allow your hands to return slowly to your sides. Do this four times. On the fourth reach, bring your arms back down quite slowly. As you do, imagine that the grapefruit have grown suddenly heavy and you have to resist having the weight pull your arms down too rapidly.

Gentle Windmill   Spread your feet comfortably apart and extend your arms to your sides. Look at your left hand, and slowly allow your eyes and hand to move toward your left rear. Return to center and do the same thing to your right. If you are comfortable with this exercise and are not putting any uncomfortable stress on your lower back, you can speed up the motion. Just make sure you stay within a comfortable reach. Do this 10 times.

Bouncing Ball   Rise up on the balls of your feet, balance on your toes as well as possible, and allow your shoulders to go limp. Keep your toes touching the ground at all times and begin bouncing. Do not allow your heels to touch the ground. Do this 10 times.

Cat's Meow Repeat the bouncing ball exercise, but this time stretch your mouth open slowly, feeling the comfortable tension of the muscles inside. Picture a kitten putting everything it has into the biggest yawn possible.

Other Techniques

There are other proven ways to reduce stress. Recite a children's rhyme or a silly quotation, gesturing excessively and broadly as you speak. Use the following breathing exercise to help improve the oxygen flow to your brain and reduce stress: Inhale only through your nose, sniffing in the air, for four counts. Hold your breath for four counts. Exhale, only through your mouth, for eight counts, pushing out all the remaining breath with the last count. Repeat the procedure twice.

As you feel your stress easing, tell yourself that you are feeling calmer. This helps to reinforce your ability to control stress and reassure your subconscious (where most learning takes place) that you are in charge of the situation.

When stress eases, the blood flow throughout the body is improved, bringing vital oxygen to the brain and enabling the mind to calm down and not send out panic signals. When the mind assumes that the whole being is safe, it no longer needs to prepare for a fight-flight response, which would be impossible during an interview. The fight-flight response may be particularly strong in a new situation such as an interview. Because it is inappropriate for you to fight with or run from the interviewer, you must either endure the emotion, learn to overcome these feelings, or suffer from increasing and intensified nervous emotions in the future.

If you feeling particularly stressful before your first interviews, burn off tension and pump up your adrenalin at the same time by bouncing on the balls of your feet, doing jumping jacks, or swinging your arms and then slapping your hands together out in front of you. Because how you stand or sit can also affect your stress levels, avoid tension by assuming confident postures and keeping your body evenly balanced. When standing, keep your feet spread slightly apart and your legs bent at the knees. When seated, keep both feet on the floor.

Do not lean on anything: leaning creates pressure, which causes muscle tension and brings about stress. Do not even shift your weight to one foot or cross your legs.

The traditional advice to keep the "chin up, stomach in, chest out, eyes straight ahead" describes the stance of a confident person, and it works. You can even improve on that advice by adding, "shoulders relaxed and jaw tension released."

The Value of Self-talk

You should monitor what your mind says to itself as you anticipate the interview. Self-talk happens three times as often as verbal conversation, and the subconscious mind tends to believe what the conscious mind tells it. Although it is normal to have negative thoughts on occasion, the more you can stop them from influencing your behavior, the more successful you will be in any situation. Making positive statements to yourself helps accelerate the process of feeling and acting confident. When you catch yourself thinking negative thoughts, replace them instantly with positive ones. If you say, "This interview is going to bomb," your subconscious will respond accordingly. Even saying, "I'm not going to bomb" is not effective since the negative word "bomb" still reaches your subconscious. Instead, concentrate your thoughts on something like, "I will be successful" or "This interview will be an opportunity to share some important points with the public."

You may need a special technique to help you stop negative thoughts and replace them with positive thoughts. Here is one especially effective technique. The instant I sense a negative thought running around in my brain, I push my thumbnail into my index finger on my left hand and mentally shout, "Stop it!" Then I silently tell my mind "Thanks, but no thanks for trying to be helpful" and quickly switch the thought to its most positive counterpart. My awareness of negative thoughts has provided me with a small callus near the tip of my index finger, happily accompanied by an encouraging abundance of positive thoughts about what I do and how I do it.

Find your own "trigger"—your personal technique for putting a halt to your negative self-talk—and develop the habit of thinking positively about yourself. If you use this technique during interviews, they will be more successful and your attitude toward them will be positive. Finally, when the situation ends, as all situations must at some point, think to yourself, "It's over. I did my best. Let me put this aside and get on with life." This acknowledgment helps release any residual stress that may remain after a difficult interview.

Try Smiling

You are in charge of your emotions. Stress is simply your mind's way of trying to help you deal constructively with whatever is confronting you. If you perceive someone as a threat, your mind will prepare you for fight or flight. Since neither would be acceptable, just change your mind about how you choose to feel.

Smiling helps. A pleasant, understanding smile—not a smirk or a grimace—can make you feel better even if you are momentarily uncomfortable with what is going on. Smiling is another way to tell the mind that you are in charge of your feelings and that it can cease any effort to prepare you for fight or flight.

Your Lasting First Impression

Research shows that people form impressions even before you say a word. Within the first 10 seconds of your media interviews, the host—always sensitive to what his or her audience will find interesting—assesses your ability to provide an interesting interview by reading your eyes, face, and body. In the first few sentences you utter, the interviewer gathers additional impressions based largely on vocal tones rather than content. Once he or she puts voice and nonverbals together, the impression has been fixed. The person who said "You never have a second chance to make a first impression" was right. You might be able to shape it a bit, but the basic impression you have created is the one that survives.

THE SEVEN C'S

If you want the interviewer and the audience to respond favorably to you from the start, practice the seven important attributes that an effective communicator should convey—calmness, confidence, competence, courtesy, caring (or consideration), cheerfulness, and creativity.

Calmness Calm guests create a feeling of ease rather than disease. They are alert, attentive, and in charge of their emotions and appear ready to handle whatever they encounter.

Confidence Confident guests do their homework. They have a reasonable idea of the topics that will be covered during the interview and have taken the time to prepare to discuss them. They know that doing their best is the most that anyone can do and that their best will fill the interviewer's needs. They exude a warm attitude and encourage the same attitude in others.

Competence Competent guests have the information that their interviewers need to conduct a good interview. They do not appear self-effacing and do not attempt to impress. Their highly developed interviewing skills give them poise.

Courtesy Courteous guests take others' needs into account. Their thoughtfulness is expressed in their attitudes and in their comments. They stay with the flow of events as they happen and participate appropriately.

Caring Caring guests are considerate. They are especially attuned to what makes others tick. They respect other people and try to help others bring out their best.

Cheerfulness Cheerful interview subjects have a positive outlook and do not become emotionally involved in others' problems. They acknowledge others' needs and desires and express interest in others' interests. They make the best of whatever comes their way, turning life's lemons into lemonade.

Creativity Creative guests seek and find ways to turn a spontaneous opportunity to everyone's advantage. They are alert to others' ideas and provide reflective feedback. They empathize with others in a variety of ways and develop good rapport with others.

Begin displaying all of these attributes *before* you begin the interview. As you travel to the interview, think about how you will display each one, and commit yourself to displaying and conveying them with each person you meet once you open the door to the building that houses the studio. Begin with your first contact with someone and continue until you leave.

ONE CLIENT'S EXPERIENCE
One client came back from an interview with this story. His topic was a positive aspect of what some might consider to be a bad-news story. Before his training he had not done well on the air. He often allowed

himself to be defensive and was about to quit doing media interviews. As he put it, he "wasn't having a very good time" with interviews.

During our session, he mastered the seven C's without coaching, so we talked a bit about maintaining the right attitude and the importance of staying true to one's self. Then we did the tapings and critiques. It was clear that his future success would be determined by having a positive attitude at all times and communicating the attributes of the seven C's. A few days after our session, he accepted an interview with a local television station.

When he arrived a half hour before air time, he exchanged pleasantries with the receptionist and noted that she said very little to anyone else who walked up to her desk. He managed to break the barrier by beginning with a friendly smile on his face. I use fictitious names here to tell the story.

He didn't ask, "Is Alysson Rohndels in?" as others did. Instead, he announced himself, using friendly voice tones that matched his warm expression: "Hi, I'm Michael Burgher and I have an appointment with Alysson Rohndels at four o'clock for a 4:15 spot on the 'Names in the News' show. Would you let her know I'm here a bit early?"

Without looking up, the receptionist said, "I'll buzz. Just have a seat." Instead, our client remained discreetly near the desk so that the receptionist could speak with him after her call: "Mr. Burgher, the producer's glad you arrived early and said she'll be out in a few minutes."

Our client thanked her and added, "It must be neat to be the first person everyone meets when they come here."

She reflected and said, "Yeah, I guess it's not so bad."

"Are you pretty busy most of the time?" he asked.

"No, more like bored. No time to really talk to anybody. You just say 10 words to somebody and 'whoosh'—they're gone." At that instant, the producer stepped into the lobby. "See what I mean?" the receptionist said. "Well, don't let the lions and tigers get you."

Our client paused at the desk, extended his hand. "Thanks for talking with me. You helped me overcome some prestage jitters."

"I hadn't thought of it that way," the receptionist added. "Well, have fun."

Our client greeted the producer with a relaxed smile and a handshake. "Thanks for coming out for me early. I thought you might have some last-minute questions or suggestions for me."

"Glad you're here. Let me explain the process." And they walked down the hall.

Our client also had a pleasant exchange with the makeup person and with another guest in the green room where they watched the host interview another guest on a monitor. When he was escorted into the studio, he walked confidently because he knew what to expect and introduced himself to the nearest camera operator, to the person who put his mike on him, and to the interviewer since they were on a commercial break.

The interview went on the air at 4:15, as scheduled, but it actually began with the first hello in the lobby. As he left, he thanked everyone briefly and walked to the lobby where the receptionist was preparing to leave for the day.

"Thanks, Ms. Petrie," he said with a smile. "The lions and tigers were friendly."

"Guess you did okay," she replied. "Come back and see us."

And he probably will be invited to do so. Knowing and practicing the seven C's paid off.

A GOAL WORTH ATTAINING

Look for the seven C's in the people you see on television. Observe the people who are most likely to interview you. Create a scorecard for them and they will suddenly become more human. Research shows that the more we know about a person, the less intimidated we are likely to be in their presence.

I periodically look at all the major interview personalities as a way to keep up with new techniques. Two are outstanding—Ted Koppel because in virtually every interview he scores at the top in all seven attributes and Larry King because although he does not rank at the top in all seven categories, he has an outstanding ability for being able to get beneath what seems to be the story and give his audiences something special.

It takes time to work on the seven C's, but it is worth the effort. The process may be unending. I recall a bumper sticker that sized this up well: "Please be patient. God's not finished with me yet." Be patient with yourself as you acquire these attributes and be patient with others who are on the same journey.

8
Getting Comfortable on Television

When you are scheduled for a television studio interview, arrive early. Become familiar with the surroundings. Your job is to be comfortable, natural, and at ease in what may be a strange and unfamiliar environment.

The pull-back shots that close news programs and talk shows may have given you an idea about what you might find on the other side of the cameras, but most people are unprepared to walk into the studio to find a large, relatively vacant area that looks nothing like what you see on your television screen at home.

Microphones are everywhere—on chairs, suspended from booms, and even hanging from the overhead lighting grids. Any one of them could be live and recording your every word. Lights are mounted overhead, and some may be on stands. Cameras seem to be everywhere, waiting to be pointed at you. When you are on the air, the red lights on top of these cameras will blink at you. A studio or floor monitor has your picture or the interviewer's on the screen as you talk. Technicians talk in the background. Crew members move sets or props. Wires cover the floor.

As other crew members wearing headsets walk around, makeup people stand by to adjust the way you look under the lights. You may see people working behind a large glass window and hear the S.A., or studio announce, which may sound like the voice of God but is actually the amplified voice of a technician speaking from the control room to the studio.

All too soon, someone clips a microphone on your clothing or, worse for the unprepared, hands the mike to you and expects you to know what to do with it. Then operators move cameras into position, a floor director gives hand signals to the host, and you are on the air.

With all of this going on—talking with someone you never have met before, seeing people do things you never have seen done before, being surrounded by equipment that may be totally unfamiliar to you—you are expected to be comfortable.

A Survival Guide to the Studio

Arriving at a television or radio studio for the first time can be an intimidating experience for the uninitiated. Television studios consist of little more than empty space filled with sets designed to approximate reality, wires, lights, and equipment. Radio studios are often small, crowded, and cluttered. You can survive this experience if you understand studio protocol, how each piece of equipment is used, and how the various people you meet play roles in the interview process.

Radio is relatively simple. The person who interviews you also may serve as the audio engineer and make the necessary equipment adjustments. You will most likely be interviewed at a table that has two mikes either mounted on table stands or suspended before you from booms. If you aren't certain how to speak into them, ask for instructions. Try to ignore the mikes once you begin, and be certain to gesture naturally. Look at the interviewer about 90 percent of the time, even when he or she may be looking elsewhere.

Television is more complex. The green room, cameras, monitors, makeup, seating, microphone countdowns, and cues all complicate the process.

GREEN ROOM
Before you enter the studio, you may be greeted and taken to a "green room"—a waiting room where you sit until you are called to go on the air. It is not necessarily green; this nomenclature is left over from early days in theater.

In this room a television set usually carries whatever program the station is sending on the air. If your interviewer is on the air, watch the TV set; if not, ignore the television, and concentrate on what you want to say in the interview.

If you are offered coffee, tea, or soft drinks, protect your throat by avoiding hot or cold drinks. Also avoid the powdered sugar donuts that many studios offer because they are greasy and could disturb your digestion on the air. Sip water or a slightly flat, carbonated beverage (no ice). If your diet permits, a few sips of a caffeinated cola might provide added stimulus.

If your interviewer is available and if time allows, meet him or her before the interview so that you feel more at ease when you are seated on the set. Caution: Inside the green room or the studio keep your comments positive. Do not discuss anything you do not want used on the air with the interviewer.

Before your interview try to see the studio and the set you will use. Shake hands with someone you meet, perhaps the floor director or a camera operator. The act of reaching out to someone helps you feel friendly and confident; at least you will know whether your voice works. A few words, such as, "Hi, I'm Jane Jones," establish the right tone and give you the assurance you need.

CAMERAS
Notice whether the set uses one, two, or three cameras. If three cameras are set up, one camera will aim over your shoulder to take close-ups of the interviewer, another will aim over your interviewer's shoulder to take close-ups of you, and the third camera will take cover shots that encompass either one or both of you.

On the set the camera with the red light (also called the talley light) flashing sends pictures over the air at that second, but you should ignore the cameras altogether. Certainly do not try to anticipate the director's plan and look at the camera you think is live. The director might call up a different shot from one of the other cameras, leaving viewers with a beautiful close-up of your earlobe.

MONITOR
The studio monitor is a television set that may be placed within a few feet of where you sit to enable the interviewer to see the shot that is on the air, and to know whether the program is in or out of commercial.

Before the program begins, you can use the monitor to check your appearance. Be aware, however, that a televised picture is not a mirror: it is a positive image. An attempt to brush your hair out of your face may find you reaching for the wrong side of your head. Once you are on the air, ignore the monitor, and avoid the temptation to look at yourself on it. The floor monitor can be distracting and even hypnotic, and watching it takes away interviewer eye contact that is vital to your success.

COUNTDOWNS AND CUES

Countdowns and other announcements may be made before and after your interview. At the start of an interview someone may say something such as, "Quiet on set. Stand by. Roll tape. Tape is rolling."

Hand signals are another potential distraction that you should learn to ignore. The floor director or someone else will be using such signals throughout the interview to tell the talent when to begin, when to end, which camera to look at, when to stretch out the interview a bit longer, when to speed it up, and so on. Again, don't let these influence you— sometimes that is easier said than done. One person I know was interviewed by a host who acknowledged cues with a nonverbal response so obvious that the guest turned to see what the host was looking at. The guest was caught looking and felt rather foolish. Once again, if you want to be in the game, you have to play by the rules of the house.

MAKEUP

You probably were offered makeup before you went into the green room, and if you were smart, you accepted it. Now that you are in the studio, allow a technician to apply more, if needed (or put it on for the first time if this was not done earlier). Lights and camera angles can distort facial features, and makeup merely restores a natural appearance for the folks at home.

If you are wearing a necktie and you feel overly warm, before you go on camera unbutton your top shirt button and then slide the tie back in place. The audience will not notice the adjustment.

Some studios are not well air conditioned. If you get hot under the lights, ask whether a crew member can "mop" you during commercials. If your interview is held outside in the sun and you begin to perspire, ask ahead of time to be mopped during breaks. Should all else fail, however, take care of any beads of perspiration on your face before they become drips. Touch the area lightly with your fingertips in a casual sweeping motion during commercials or when someone else is talking and you're certain you're not on camera. You may need to practice a few times before you feel comfortable doing this, but the perspiration could convey a negative message.

SEATING

When you take your seat for the interview, always choose a chair rather than a sofa. Ask for one as a substitute, if necessary. Just say, "I'd feel more comfortable in a chair. Would it be possible to have one?" The answer will either be yes or no.

Once you have a seat, check to see whether it is so low or deep that it is uncomfortable. If so, ask for a cushion to sit on or place behind you, or ask for a more comfortable seat.

If the chair rocks, rolls, or swivels, it will allow you to transmit nervous energy through its motion, distracting the audience from your message and making you appear nervous or lacking in self-control. Resolve to keep your chair still at all times. You can even ask the crew to tape the swivel, rocking mechanism, or wheels (particularly if the chair is placed near the edge of a riser).

If your feet don't reach the floor when you sit down, ask the crew to place a small platform or a cushion under them—as long as they agree to not show it in the shots that they put on the air. If your legs are long and the seat is low, ask to have the chair elevated a few inches on a platform so you can put your feet comfortably on the floor. Again, ask that this adaptation not be shown in the shots used on the air.

When you sit, slide toward the front part of the chair, making certain you don't cut the circulation behind your knees. Avoid the Lincoln Memorial position—sitting squarely with your hands gripping both arms of the chair. Instead, turn your body about 30 degrees off center and face the interviewer—even if you have to twist your chair slightly away from the interviewer to assume this posture. This position enables you to drop your hands and arms to your lap where you will be less tempted to white-knuckle the arms of your chair. It also frees them up for gestures and provides interesting camera shots for the director to use on the air.

Don't be tempted to lean back in the comfortable position you might assume at home or in your office. On television this comes across as too relaxed and may convey the impression that the interview is not important to you. This semi-reclining position also inhibits good breathing and proper voice production. Instead, lean in toward the interviewer. This communicates your interest and involvement in the interview and shows you can meet the interviewer eye to eye. From a technical standpoint, leaning in also helps the director get a tighter picture when he or she needs two heads in one shot.

MICROPHONES

"What do I do with the microphone?" is a question many television guests ask. In most studios, the crew "dresses" or attaches the mike for you. If, however, no one assists, ask for help if you need it. Take your cues from your interviewers: if they put on their own mikes, you may be expected to do so as well. Attaching the mike is a relatively simple task but can contribute to nervousness if you try doing it without practice and find yourself fumbling. As noted earlier, most studio mikes are clip-ons, but a few studios still use mikes with cords that go around the neck. Handle them carefully: $300 and up is not an uncommon price for one of these little devices.

Cord Mikes   When you put on a cord mike, leave the cord attached so that it continues to form a loop. Slide one end of the cord down, much as you would a tie in a neckerchief slide, and slip the open loop over your head, being careful not to disturb your hair. With the cord around your neck, tighten it until you have the microphone about a handspan beneath your chin or about an inch above pocket height. This position enables the audio technician to get a good voice level.

Clip-on Mikes   If you are given a clip mike, regard it like a tie clasp with a small ornament mounted on the front of it. Open the clip and fasten it with the ornament (mike) facing outward. Attach it to a necktie, the fold of your jacket lapel, or blouse or shirt lapel if you are wearing neither a jacket nor a tie. If you have a choice, affix the mike so that it is on the side of you that is closer to the interviewer. Conceal the excess wire. The powerpack for wireless miles may have to be clipped to your belt or waistband.

Mounted Mikes   In most radio station studios guests are seated, and the microphone is mounted on a table stand in front of you, and in some radio studios the mike is suspended from a boom. In either case, keep your hands away from it. If the mike is on a table stand, do not tap or bump the table.

If you are interviewed standing in front of a mike, the microphone may be mounted on an adjustable floor stand and should be placed a few inches below your chin. However, in most standing interviews the interviewer holds the microphone in his or her hand. Do not be intimidated into backing away when the interviewer thrusts the mike toward you: it needs to be held close to pick up your voice properly while screening out other sounds, so stand your ground.

An interviewer who holds the mike may use a speed-up technique. If the reporter pulls the microphone away from you before you finish each response, make it a point to finish your replies and to do so at your own pace. Also watch for the stall technique, in which the reporter leaves the mike in front of you after you finish your answer. When this happens, either stop talking, or score positive points for your organization or cause.

Mike Check   When you are asked to do a mike check, the technician wants to determine your voice level for recording or transmission. The check can be stressful to the unprepared. Generally, someone such as an audio engineer or technician will say, "Can we get a level on the guest?" They are asking you to speak long enough to allow them to make the proper settings on their equipment. Don't say "Testing, one-two-three"; technicians generally need one or two sentences to set the levels. Instead, say something that will help both you and the interviewer begin positively. Say your name, pronouncing it carefully so the interviewer will hear it, then give your position and your organization's name, and cap that off with the most positive point you can make about the subject you are there to discuss. Do this in five seconds or less. For example: "I'm John Jones, chief executive officer of the XYZ Company, which has had a remarkable safety record over the past 10 years." During your check, the audio technician may signal for you to stop, which means that he or she has heard enough to adjust the levels. Finish your sentence but keep it brief.

More on Microphones   In some radio and television studios mikes are always active. Your picture may not be going out over the air, but the crew may be recording everything you say. I believe that once you step inside the studio, anything you say is fair game—and evidently a number of stations feel that way, too.

If you are wearing a wireless mike and leave the room or studio during breaks, shut off the mike. Otherwise your every comment may be broadcast back into the studio over the S.A., which is like a public address system.

Intercoms   Camera operators often use portable two-way communications systems—sometimes even as your interview is taking place. The microphones you use on the set are unidirectional, and the gains, or volumes, are set for close pickup only, so no one else will hear crew voices. Ignore them, and focus on the interview.

Your Gestures and Posture

Gestures are extremely important to a television interview. People who watch you on television are looking for an interesting program, and gestures help make that possible. They help you to bring more of your personality into the situation.

The more you can do with your posture and gestures to contribute to a visually interesting program, the more appreciative the television audience will be. Gesturing provides viewers with moving pictures rather than boring, talking heads that might cause them to switch channels.

WHEN YOU INHIBIT GESTURES
People tend to gesture less when they are first interviewed on television than they do in everyday conversation. In any new or strange environment, our instinct for self-preservation tends to inhibit all of our actions—and for most people a television studio is unfamiliar.

During an interview, however, nervous energy always finds an outlet. It must go somewhere, and gesturing channels this nervous energy constructively. If you do not gesture, you may find yourself clinging to your chair, adjusting your clothing or eyeglasses, stroking your hair, picking at lint, at food stains, at loose fabric on the arm of your chair, at knots in the mike cord, and even at facial blemishes, fiddling with coffee cups or water glasses, scratching anything that seems to itch at the moment, and playing with microphone cords, rings or other jewelry, and even with your fingers. In standing interviews, you are likely to put your hands in and out of your pockets or lock your hands firmly together and end up gesturing with your head. Many people in my media-interviewing seminars are shocked when they watch the initial videotaped replays of what they did with their hands on camera.

Your hands also can't work for you if you grip your knees or the arms of your chair or if you lock them together or use one hand to hold down the other. In a seated interview, rest them lightly and loosely on your legs with your thumbs turned slightly up. This frees them to gesture when you need them to. Keep this rule in mind: hands that face down tend to stay down; hands that face up tend to go up. In a standing interview, think of them as "hot hands": every time they touch each other, you could get burned, so you have to wave them around to cool them off.

It is to your benefit to use your gestures as soon as possible, even if you force the first few just to prime the pump and allow other gestures to come naturally.

FORCED GESTURES

Once the interview begins, however, make certain your motions are congruent with your *e*-motions. Planned or forced gestures always come late. By the time the mind consciously thinks to gesture, picks one, and then tells the body to carry it out, the mouth has already spoken the words that should have accompanied the gesture. Mechanical gestures always occur about a beat too late and make you look foolish. Work on this in rehearsal: decide ahead of time what emotions should accompany your words, experience those emotions, and then allow the appropriate gestures to occur naturally.

Gestures help you communicate in many ways: they add enthusiasm and other positive emotions to your voice, making you sound more interesting, and punctuate the messages you deliver. In fact, if you lock your hands together and don't gesture, either your head will bob distractingly, or your responses will tend to lack enthusiasm. When that happens, the interviewer's concern for ratings may cause him or her to take whatever steps are needed to add some zip to the program. This could include techniques that might fire up your emotions, but in a negative way.

A REMINDER

If you still are reluct to gesture, remember that 55 percent of your total message comes through your body language and 38 percent comes through your voice—which is aided by your gestures. (Is this beginning to sound familiar?) If you want to communicate the remaining 7 percent of your message—the content portion—to the audience, it is a good idea to pay close attention to this overwhelming 93 percent. There is no room for debate on this one: natural gestures that spring from genuine emotions are essential to any interview.

YOUR LEGS

How you position your legs during a seated interview is important. Crossing them tends to push you back in the chair, inhibit your breathing, and cut off circulation. If you cross them and point your foot away from the host, your body language—exaggerated by television—says you are blocking the interviewer and makes you appear defensive. Cross them the opposite way in the tight quarters of many television studio sets and you may find your foot against the interviewer's knee.

Two positions work best and are comfortable for most people: the semi-starter's position with legs together and one foot slightly in front of the other as though you were about to run a race, or the finishing-school position with legs crossed lightly at the ankles. Both are suitable for men and women.

Avoid the splayed-legs position at all costs. From a head-on camera angle, it looks worse than it does in real life no matter how you're dressed.

EYE CONTACT

Where to look during the interview is another concern for most guests. The answer is to look directly at the interviewer as much as 90 percent of the total time you are being interviewed. If you're a bit uncomfortable with this degree of eye contact, shift your focus to the interviewer's ear, forehead, nose, or chin from time to time. You should not look away, however.

The interviewer appreciates a guest's eye contact because it helps block out studio distractions and enables the guest to concentrate on the question at hand, which, in turn, leads to a more interesting program.

Eye contact also can help you to relax if you feel uneasy. It conveys an attitude to the audience (and to your subconscious) that you and the interviewer are equals—that you can meet him or her eye to eye.

During your interview, the tougher the questions you are asked, the more important your eye contact becomes. The air of confidence it conveys enhances your credibility with the audience at home.

Because a television image is two-dimensional, viewers see only part of you on the flat television screens in their living rooms. They see nothing above you, so your breaking eye contact with the interviewer can produce unfortunate effects. If you look up to think, especially after a tough question, it looks to the home viewers as though you are looking for divine guidance—as in "Dear God, please help me." If you look down after a tough question, it appears as though you are prayerfully seeking help. Sidewards glances are also taboo: they make you look as though you are seeking the quickest escape route.

A good rule of thumb is to look at the person who is speaking or to whom you are speaking, even when that person is not looking at you—especially when there are more than two people on the program. When the interviewer is looking at the camera (talking directly to the audience at home) at the opening or closing of the program, or when going into or coming out of a commercial, don't allow a camera to catch you gazing around, checking out the light grid, or adjusting your mike. You will look uninterested or even foolish. You can break eye contact briefly during your own responses, but even then be aware of the risks.

SPECIFIC GESTURES AND POSTURES
The human body can transmit thousands of nonverbal signals. The muscles around the eyes and mouth combine to form dozens of messages, and they are added to the many different postures that can be assumed by the head, neck, shoulders, back, arms, and legs. If you multiply each position of each part by all the combinations possible with each other part, the numbers are staggering.

Of course, you could drive yourself to distraction if you attempted to monitor these in an interview, assign meaning to them, and then act on what you have concluded. Rather than isolating any part of the body and attempting to draw meaning from whatever it is doing, consider individuals' nonverbals in specific situations and in context with whatever is transpiring. Consider the total of people's signaling body parts such as eyes, mouth, neck, shoulders, back, arms, legs, and their overall body postures such as standing erect versus slumping. Again, there are no absolutes, and context and intent will dictate interpretation.

Your Convictions

Television sets are found in living rooms, family rooms, bedrooms, and even kitchens and bathrooms. It is an intimate medium, indeed, and the people who appear on TV talk with their audiences in conversational tones, the way Donahue talks with them every morning over coffee.

Because television is a medium that involves its viewers on more than one level, you need to put more of yourself into your appearances than you do during a print interview. A print reporter may try to convey his or her impressions of how you come across during the interview, but television viewers see and hear you for themselves.

During your interviews, you may speak in fragmentary and choppy sentences, in part, because of the stress of the interview, the pace, or your reflection of the interviewer's own style. Since this is consistent with normal conversation, don't be concerned about it. It is far better to communicate this way than to try to speak in complete sentences and paragraphs that come across as sounding rehearsed and insincere.

By now you've probably realized that much of television is a game. Very little of what takes place through this medium is real. With its fake living rooms made of propped-up flats, its time compression that tries to simulate real conversation, its excessive lights to enable its cameras to read your image, its effort to hide microphones that capture your voice, and its use of makeup to restore your natural look, interviewing *is* a game. Your only concern should be how to play it to win so that no one loses.

DEALING WITH BOREDOM

When you do a number of interviews on the same topic, you may become bored with your own words. This has to do with frame of mind more than anything else and need not happen. I probably have repeated many of this book's techniques a thousand times or more. Yet I still share them with enthusiasm because they are fresh and new to my clients and I enjoy seeing them learn each technique and find how well it works for them. If you tire of repeating the same messages, put yourself in the other person's place each time you interview and you should overcome the problem.

If you find nonwords like *um* and *ah* creeping into your interviews, focus on your bottom line—the positive point you wish to make—before you begin to answer the question and then respond at a smooth and even pace.

Get in touch with the significance of what you are saying. If you look and sound bored, the interviewer is almost compelled to either end your segment or heat up the action so viewers don't change channels. Even if you do stay on the air, the impression of boredom that you convey is not a good one. You can't afford to sound bored about important topics because the audience sees and hears the conflict and draws conclusions that will not serve your best interests or your organization's.

Conveying Your Convictions

In your televised interviews, you need to convey your feelings and emotions with dignity and professionalism. After all, you are going to be less than 10 feet away from most viewers—in their homes. You can't *afford* to be a dud if you want them to like and accept you and your cause.

Let them know how you feel and also how you want *them* to feel. "I'm angry," said one of our clients with strong conviction in his voice and body language in a live, televised interview. Then he added, "And you should be angry, too." The interviewer wondered why and said so out loud, giving our client the opportunity he needed to give the entire viewing audience the justification they needed to share this emotion.

Most researchers say that people have only six *basic* emotions and that only one of these—happiness—can be regarded as positive. Four—anger, disgust, fear, and sadness—are clearly negative, and the final one, surprise, can go either way.

These are the basic emotions and thousands more can be displayed, which certainly indicates the need to work hard to convey positive feelings and emotions during interviews. Most other expressions—such as expressions of confidence, openness, and cooperation—are determined by cultural and environmental factors in both the sending and the receiving. For example, Americans recognize that when someone forms his or her thumb and index finger into a circle, they are sending an "okay" symbol. However, in Latin and South America, the same gesture is considered obscene.

Emotions should be allowed to be expressed naturally. Feelings should be experienced before their physical expression. Using the so-called right gestures, postures, and expressions too early conveys an impression of incongruity. You have a better chance of communicating when you say the right words with the right voice tones—convince people that you believe what you say.

Late gestures often stem from a sudden need to force fit a gesture to underscore a point. Most often, the effort comes across as insincere.

Emotions that help viewers associate positive feelings with your message include your hopes, beliefs, ambitions, care, concern, confidence, trust, stability, generosity, sense of humor, poise, and so on. Use these emotions to clarify points and convey credibility.

You also can use your voice, gestures, eye contact, and voice tones to express such emotions as empathy, compassion, understanding, concern, generosity, courtesy, caring, and cooperation.

With practice, you can use your emotions to persuade, counsel, and reassure. You also can use them to challenge ideas rather than individuals and to convey a feeling of teamwork—an attitude that says "We're all in this together." By mastering your own feelings, you can better understand the other person's and "walk in his or her moccasins" until you reach a mutually acceptable destination.

NO DEBATES

Understanding your own emotions and observing others' can help you avoid debates with interviewers or other guests on a panel discussion. When you find yourself facing potential hostility, immediately attack the issue rather than the person who raised it. Although in a heated television or radio interview you may not have time to use what I call defusers, such as, "If I were in your position, I might be inclined to agree," you should try to express an attitude of tolerance and respect with every muscle in your body.

Unfortunately, unless you've rehearsed and have learned how to remain cool when the person roleplaying the opponent rattles your cage, you aren't ready to use defusers. You need to be totally desensitized to potential triggers before you can react with confident control in a heated situation—especially one that is coupled with the stress of an interview.

This doesn't mean you shouldn't match the challenger's emotions, hot as they may be; in fact, you should, as we'll see in a moment. You do have to direct your energies into constructive communication that helps you both. Let's say an interviewer has been roughing you up and then escalates matters further with avoidance (active) body language and voice tones and demands of you: "Then why *don't* you clean up the environment? Why don't you stop spending all your money on executive perks? Why don't you admit you run a dirty operation?"

To respond with a "Let's-all-calm-down" attitude is unlikely to send positive messages to the audience and may make you appear like a placater who can't take it, or a wimp. You don't, however, want to attack the interviewer—whose familiar face appears daily or weekly in the homes of your audience. Instead, you should match the intensity, the voice tones, and the gestures and direct your full energy to the issue: "We have a clean operation, we've won environmental awards at this plant, and I'm proud of the people who work here." Zap! No one is hurt, and you come across as steadfast in your convictions and willing to let the world know how you feel—a pretty good outcome for a response of less than four seconds.

Attack interviewers and the audience is with *them*. Attack issues and you at least keep the door open for audiences to accept your viewpoint. Most of all, you've matched emotion with emotion in a positive and healthy way. It works—and for all the right reasons. Rather than cause you to expend your emotions on negative feelings, this approach enables you to express them positively. Negatives tend to drain you, but positives tend to envigorate you: you feel even more confident each time you respond accordingly.

CUB REPORTERS

Fortunately, most of your interviews will not be intensely stressful, particularly once you know what to expect and how to respond. Of greater concern at the local level is that you will be dealing not with reporters who know all the tricks but with those who don't know enough of them. Lack of knowledge or skills, irresponsibility, ignorance, or laziness are all real concerns when dealing with reporters and interviewers at the local level. Many believe that home-town reporters generate stories that do more damage to a reputation than a tough interview by a pro at the national level. Although in print journalism at the local level the work of the cub reporter (or even the newspaper's best and most experienced person for the job) is subject to the professional hand of a seasoned editor, even that person may be unfamiliar with the issues or may not have time to question the story. Thus, you may have to ensure that your words and motives cannot be misinterpreted when the story is written.

A live radio or television interview at the local level may be a safer bet than a print interview. At least it goes right out over the airwaves and no one can edit you. In this environment, only you have control over the message the audience receives. Tape, however, is another story (see chapter 15).

Preparing for the Interview

When you know you are going to be interviewed on television, watch the program beforehand. Become familiar with the show's format or sequence of events. Observe the interviewer's style: is he or she aggressive, inquisitive, helpful, negative, laid back?

   Learn as much as possible about how the interviewer regards your industry, your organization, and the issue you are there to discuss. Ask how long the interview will last and the general area of inquiry. Be prepared to turn negative questions or interview techniques into positive responses.

   Being comfortable on television comes through planning and preparing well in advance. When Eliot Frankel interviewed me for a *Washington Journalism Review* article ("Learning to Conquer 'Mike Fright,'" July-August 1982), I said that executives owe it to their organizations to spend a few hours preparing for the Mike Wallaces of the broadcast business. Wallace agreed, saying, "It makes perfect sense to me because people should have every opportunity to make the best case they can for themselves."

   The same article quoted Irving Shapiro, then chairman and chief executive officer of DuPont, whom I had counseled to appear on "The Donahue Show": "You wouldn't drive a car without practicing, and when you go into the world of professional TV you ought to know what the experience is like. If you don't know that, you're at a huge disadvantage."

   One final tip: read the daily newspaper in the city where you will be interviewed. The interviewer may read it and have questions for you—often based on articles that relate to your interview in seemingly remote ways.

Important Points to Remember

Attitude is everything. Viewers judge you by your postures, facial expressions, and voice tones even more than by what you say.

Television is a medium of impressions, and the first impression the audience forms of you is likely to be the one that stays with them. In any situation, the first 10 percent of your total interview time produces

---

Irving Shapiro, Former chairman and CEO, DuPont

   You wouldn't drive a car without practicing, and when you go into the world of professional TV you ought to know what the experience is like. If you don't know that, you're at a huge disadvantage.

the audience's lasting impression of you. On television, this becomes even more critical since you may only appear on camera for a few minutes.

Since you're a guest in viewers' homes and they often regard the interviewer as a friend, be friendly and conversational. Use the interviewer's name.

During a seated interview, sit toward the front of the chair, lean forward at a slight angle. Cross your legs at the ankles or place one foot in front of the other. Remain still. Don't rock or swivel.

Gestures help to reduce stress. To keep your hands available to gesture, rest them lightly on your legs, facing slightly up.

Good eye contact is essential. Regardless of where the cameras are positioned, keep almost constant eye contact with the interviewer—especially during brief interviews.

Smile at every logical opportunity. A genuinely felt smile dispels your tension and helps relax everyone. Even tough interviewers like to see friendly faces before them.

Part Three
The Interview

9
Dealing with the News Media's Questions

Just as you begin to get a handle on how to succeed in an interview, there is more to learn. Let's proceed by considering how an interviewer might position your segment by his or her opening comments.

Seven Interview Openers

Many interviewers attempt to add sparkle to their segments beginning with the opening credits. In fact, they use a device that can make or break an interview (or a guest): the purpose of the opening statement, or "grabber," is to keep audiences tuned in.

Several years ago, my good friend Ronald N. Levy, president of North American Precis Syndicate, Inc., listed 10 powerful openings for speakers. With his permission, I have modified these to come up with the seven that I have found interviewers are most likely to use when they kick off an interview. Let's say Alonzo Murchison of the Avid Company is about to be interviewed about his firm's intention to close its local plant. Here are seven possible openers to that interview:

- *Question the listener or viewer.* "How would you like to be in this dilemma? If you keep your plant open, the board of supervisors will shut you down for violations. If you *don't,* up to 500 people might lose their jobs. That's the situation our first guest faces today. We'll be back to talk with Alonzo Murchison of the Avid Company right after these messages."

- *Start with a historical reference.* "When the Avid Company opened its doors 40 years ago, it promised us that they would be "here forever." Now it seems they have their bags packed and—well, so much for promises. We'll be back with Alonzo Murchison of the Avid Company right after these messages."

- *Offer the "inside story."* "Perhaps you've wondered why the truck traffic has been constantly declining on Cedar Street over the past few years. Well, what may seem like good news to some of us may be a double-edged sword. We'll tell you why when we talk with Alonzo Murchison of the Avid Company right after these messages."

- *Make a prediction.* "Before today's program is over, some of you are going to be up in arms—some because the board of supervisors wants the Avid Company to keep its plant open, others because the company plans to shut its doors and walk away. We'll be back with our guest, Alonzo Murchison of the Avid Company, right after these messages."

- *Begin with a quote.* " 'We're here to stay,' promised the Avid Company when special legislation allowed them to begin operations in this community—in good faith—some 40 years ago. Now that promise will soon be broken. Perhaps our guest this morning, Alonzo Murchison of the Avid Company, can tell us why—right after these messages."

- *"Even as we speak."* "We're going to be speaking with Alonzo Murchison of the Avid Company this morning. And even as we speak, his company is packing its bags to leave town. We'll ask Mr. Murchison to tell us why—right after these messages."

- *Make a promise.* "If you are concerned about the decline of jobs in this area, you will want to know what the Avid Company is doing to help those whom they plan to lay off during the next six months. In our next segment, we'll have Alonzo Murchison of the Avid Company tell us how to deal with that concern. But first, these messages."

Don't respond to negative grabbers, especially by refuting the charges that the opener may imply. Doing so calls even further attention to the charges and wastes valuable time you need to score your own points—particularly in this interview. It may comfort you to know that most grabbers are straightforward attention getters that do no harm. Identifying these negative grabbers, however, can help you anticipate them and avoid being caught by surprise by your interviewer.

Keep in mind that in news-media interviews reporters ask the questions and guests answer them. While you are still polishing the basic skills with the techniques covered in this book, the way you answer questions—particularly in radio and television interviews—will be the clearest determinant of your success. Questions are opportunities: there are no bad questions, only the possibility of bad answers (from those who haven't prepared properly).

Reporters and Objectivity

With each interview, try to determine the reporter's personal agenda— his or her reasons for wanting to do the story or interview. This helps you decide how to focus your responses appropriately because objectivity cannot be counted on in any interview. Any hint of objectivity ceases from the moment the story is selected from among the hundreds, or even thousands, that might have been chosen. It is further removed by the aspect chosen for its focus and, finally, all but eliminated by the way the story is covered—the questions chosen, the responses that are selected, how they are positioned in relationship to other editorial comments, and even where the story appears among others in the same broadcast or on the same printed page.

SELLING NEWSPAPERS
When reporters ask questions, they are trying to anticipate their audiences: "that's what sells newspapers." Billions of dollars are at stake. They want to know what they can extract from your answers that may have value or interest to their audiences. It's all part of establishing ratings and reputations.

Each time you answer a question, the interviewer may think, "So what?" or "Who cares?" or "What's in this for my audience?" If you work at being interesting and informative and establish rapport with your interviewers, you may never have to face some of the questioners' techniques that arise when the reporter feels that an interview is not going well.

WHEN INTERVIEWERS TRY TO MANIPULATE
Some interviewers use aggressive tactics as a matter of style. They're part of their routine. They ask leading questions or loaded questions, give you forced choices, attempt to put words in your mouth, and ask hypothetical or speculative questions. Others use these tactics only

when quotable statements are not forthcoming from the guest in any other way.

Reporters try to make the interview interesting to their audiences in the best way they know how. These techniques work, in part, because guests are frequently anxious, stressful, and unprepared. Because they perceive interviewers as being in power or control, they are easily manipulated by them.

The best approach is to deal with these possibilities before they occur—by knowing your subject well enough to handle an interview successfully and by knowing how to respond to the interviewer's needs and the techniques he or she might employ to conduct a good interview.

WHAT INTERVIEWERS NEED

Interviewers seek drama and conflict and expect short, simple answers to their questions. They also appreciate responses that are entertaining as well as informative. You need to structure your answers to fulfill these needs. When what you say satisfies the interviewer, you both will be more comfortable with the interview. As we have also seen, body language and voice tones reflect the level of rapport between you. If you both feel good about the process and both of you give and receive what you need from the exchange, there is even less likelihood that an interviewer will employ any elicitive or baiting techniques.

MAINTAINING CONTROL DURING INTERVIEWS

No matter what interviewers do, you are in charge of *you*. Keep your own pace, and remain patient and calm. Always try to help achieve understanding: never become antagonistic toward the interviewer. At any sign of anger, interviewers and their audiences will wonder how you might handle more critical matters and how much of your message is based on emotion rather than on fact.

Use each question as an opportunity to show that you are a courteous and cooperative guest who is willing to share your knowledge of the subject. Maintain this attitude and you can learn to handle interview questions even more.

STAY ON THE RECORD

Some questions might cause you to want to speak off the record, say "No comment," or repeat negative charges. My rule on this is a simple one: never speak off the record to anyone—especially (and obviously) not during a live radio or television interview—regardless of how well you know the individual. Over time, reporters tend to forget what they were supposed to have kept confidential.

For those who have had a lot of successful interview experiences, there is an exception to this rule: When you know how to do it, you can leak information through reporters who are not likely to respect your off-the-record ground rules or may interpret them to mean that they should seek the same information elsewhere—which is becoming a common reaction these days.

"NO COMMENT" ANSWERS
Never say "No comment." It has come to imply an automatic self-indictment—that a person who uses this response has something to hide. No-comment answers are tantamount to invoking your fifth amendment rights.

If you cannot comment on a question, explain why and offer to inform the person when circumstances change (say, when a legal action is resolved and your hands are no longer tied). You should then offer the interviewer different information on the topic that is of equal or greater value. If, for instance, you can't provide a figure for competitive reasons, you might say, "I wish I could share that information with you, (questioner's name), but you can understand that our competitors would like it even more. But what I can tell you is this" (and provide an industry figure or a number that is not proprietary). Cap off your answer, of course, with a positive point.

WHEN ASKED NEGATIVE QUESTIONS
Never repeat a negative: people tend to remember whatever gets repeated. If you are asked, "So, I guess your company is guilty," don't respond with "No, we're not guilty." That response repeats the word *guilty* and also contains two negator words—*no* and *don't*. The conscious mind tends to drop negator words as having little or no value, leaving *guilty* standing alone and spoken for the second time—this time, from your own mouth. It may be difficult to believe, but by the end of a week people who hear denial statements tend to recall hearing something about guilt but do not know exactly what.

Use only positive words. Make only positive points. Convey only a positive attitude.

WHEN YOU DON'T KNOW
If you don't know the answer to a question, say so and offer to provide the interviewer with the information at a later time. In an on-air inter-

view where you will not have the opportunity to respond later, the audience interprets your action as courteous and cooperative. Once you're off the air, follow through with your promise—in writing. This further boosts your credibility with the reporter even though he or she may not use your letter after the story is finished.

Once you've given your "don't know" response, move on. Don't elaborate: it is better to show wisdom in your silence than ignorance in your pronouncements.

TO GAIN TIME TO THINK

Interviews are fast-paced, but a complicated or complex question may cause you to want time to think. Don't use obvious stalls for time, such as "That's a good question" or "That's a good point" or "I'm glad you asked that question" or "I'm glad you brought that up"—especially when there is absolutely no reason for you to be glad. Avoid hackneyed cliches. Answer the question, don't comment on its existence. In fact, since reporters ask questions as part of their profession, it is inappropriate to critique their questioning skill.

When reporters hear one of these stalls, they may wonder about the other questions they have asked. If they decide that you did not regard other questions highly, they may return to probe those areas of questioning or conclude that you were uncomfortable with the area they were pursuing earlier and decide to dig back into that. Some reporters who feel that you are stalling may press even harder.

To collect your thoughts, you can gain two full seconds by just remaining silent, one second by using the reporter's name, and three additional seconds by saying, "Let's see what's at issue here," or by repeating the question or by asking the reporter to repeat it—as long as the repetition will not reinforce something negative.

Avoid using such prefaces as, "Well, as I said before," or "I thought I answered that question already, but": these may give you an extra split second to think, but they come across as rude to interviewers and their audiences. Such phrases seem to imply, "Why didn't you listen the first time?" In all your responses, avoid negative words, technical jargon, or words and phrases the may be unfamiliar to the audience.

When You Face Stressful Questioning

No matter how well you have prepared, you may find yourself in situations where you are under pressure—perhaps in crisis interviews or during interviews in which you face others whose views oppose your own. In your negotiations for the interview, try to secure agreement that the interviewer's lead will position the story in what you feel is a fair and accurate manner. You can do this only if you know the topic scheduled for discussion, the manner it will be treated, and other guests to be interviewed on this subject—before you, with you, or after you.

EXPECTING THE WORST

If you anticipate an aggressive interview, try to reconcile potential differences beforehand. If the reporter is aggressive in pre-interview discussions, stay calm and remain so. There is no reason to be upset.

When your information is solid and your attitude is right, even reporters whose views are contrary to your own are doing you a favor by interviewing you: they tell you what they believe to be true and give you the opportunity to share your views with others. Your responses should reflect this: build on common bonds and ideas shared, and minimize differences as much as possible. Because there may be little time to establish areas of mutual agreement, simply state your points and allow the interviewer to draw the conclusions.

When you are on the air, listen carefully if the interviewer makes a point you can't refute. You might have to say, "We have a different way of looking at this" or "I appreciate your right to hold a different viewpoint," and then express your point without contradicting what he or she has said. If you can agree with the reporter's point (or at least the issue behind the point), do so and then bridge to a positive point of your own. This helps maintain rapport, enhance your credibility, and cultivate audience empathy.

During the interview, you can drop in brief comments on any statements the reporter makes that agree with your view or indicate a common interest, such as, "Since we share this in common" or "I'm glad we agree on this issue." Then get on with your answer at once. Debating an interviewer or another guest may lead to a hot interview, but the outcome is seldom worth the effort. If not handled perfectly, it damages the image you hope to convey and provides critics with an opportunity for extended discussion of points that you would prefer to move away from.

PROPER POSITIONING

Your response to the opening question should position you clearly. Let's say the interviewer sets the stage, introduces you, and asks, "Mr. Brentzen, just exactly why do you oppose the proposed XYZ legislation?" Your response should be something like this: "Tom, I appreciate the opportunity to comment on why we believe the XYZ legislation would be bad for the citizens of this area. It is income discriminatory, restrictive of new development, and inhibitory of further expansion of the services we know we all need."

In two opening sentences—less than 30 seconds into the interview—you've made your point on the record and set the agenda for the discussion. Any reporter who "goes with the flow"—and most do if the direction serves their needs—will be likely to pursue the subtopics you have laid on the table for further discussion. Only an extremely astute opponent could avoid feeding into the agenda you have set.

If an interviewer or another guest turns the tables on you and uses a similar technique to set the agenda, simply respond with an agenda of your own. Suppose, for example, that the other person opened with the preceding remark and that the interviewer turned to you, introduced you, and said, "Ms. Robstar, how do you respond to the accusation that your group, in effect, is supporting legislation that discriminates and restricts progress by inhibiting new development?"

You could respond with something like this: "Well, Tom, I'm glad to have the opportunity to express why we feel the proposed bill would actually cause serious economic hardship to taxpayers who would have to underwrite the costs of new roads, sewage-treatment plants, and services. We believe the XYZ proposal offers a sound alternative." You have successfully removed yourself from playing defense. Remember the sports analogy: you can't score if you don't have the ball.

As you go off the air, thank the interviewer for providing you with the opportunity to be there. Don't do as one guest is purported to have done: when the host said, "We've enjoyed having you," the guest smiled nervously and replied in a hesitant whisper, "I think I've *been* had." Remember: When you face opposition, always acknowledge the issue, find areas on which you can agree, at least in part, and then go on to make your point.

10
Interviewers' Techniques

When interviewers ask questions, they use specific techniques to elicit responses. I'm not certain whether any journalism school teaches these techniques or tells students how and when to employ them, but if any did, they would do so without intending to train interviewers to manipulate their guests' responses.

The techniques discussed in this chapter do exist and are used in local and national interviews daily across the country. Most often, interviewers use them to obtain information, and they generally use them when the speaker appears to be unprepared, uncooperative, unskilled, or boring. Even the best-coached and best-prepared guests are exposed to some of these techniques from time to time. Notice that this chapter turns each interviewing technique into a positive point. Just as it is the interviewer's job to get the story told, it is your job to tell it in the most honest and ethical way that serves your best interests. In fact, if you deny self interest or fail to act in your own behalf, reporters may find your responses suspect.

Needling

- *Example* "Really, Mr. Bentzner, do you honestly think the American public is going to buy that?"
- *Response* Stick by your guns. Don't equivocate or vacillate. Say, "Absolutely, Frank," and then go on to reinforce the positive point you've just made or make a new one.

101

False Facts (Unintentional or Deliberate)

- *Example*   "So this means your plant is no longer in compliance with the regulation. In that case, what next?"
- *Response*   Avoid the tendency to respond as though the interviewer's statements are accurate. If you know the statement is wrong, correct it graciously. Say, "On the contrary, Tess. We are in total compliance, as a matter of fact." Then go on to make a positive point about how well you comply with the regulations that cover this. If you don't know for certain whether the reporter is inaccurate, say so, but add that it doesn't sound right to you and immediately add that you therefore are unable to comment on it. If the reporter persists, ask him or her to name the source so you can check out the information and report back. This should shut this unproductive line of questioning, keep you out of a trap, and still enable you to show cooperation.

Reinterpretation of Your Response

- *Example*   "So this is not going to serve the public good, after all. Right?"
- *Response*   Avoid interpretations that are not consistent with your own words. In this case, first pause, and then say, "Lynne, we're saying that it will not enable a small segment of the public to gain more than their fair share any longer." Then go directly to your own point and end on a positive note.

Putting Words in Your Mouth

- *Example*   "So what you're saying is that you think the president's approach is wrong?"
- *Response*   Recognize that to repeat these words is to add credence to them even when you repeat them as part of a denial. Never use words you don't like, and don't argue with the questioner. Instead, say, "On the contrary, Lou, as we see the issue, the correct approach should be" (and go on to make your positive point).

False Assumption or Conclusion

- *Example*   "So, once you get the subsidy, you'll raise prices again, right?"
- *Response*   Call the technique for what it is. Say, "Well, Mark, that's an assumption I don't believe we should make" or "I don't think I agree with your conclusion, Mark." Then go on to make your positive point.

Hypothetical Premise

- *Example*   "What would happen if your department can't find the people it needs to work overtime? Won't the streets become even more dangerous?"
- *Response*   Call the shot, but watch your voice tones. "Since that's a hypothetical question, Trina, we really don't know what would happen. However, I can tell you that we are actively recruiting the force we need and we hope to have that in place by the end of the month. That would eliminate costly overtime and put us in a much better position."

Baiting You into Accusations

- *Example*   "That was a pretty dirty trick that your opponent pulled, wasn't it? How do you respond to such an individual?"
- *Response*   As we've already noted, when you wrestle with a pig, you both end up full of mud. Don't play the game. Instead of demeaning the opposition, say, "Bob, only that individual can speak for her actions. If you talk with her directly, I feel you might get a better understanding of that. However, I can tell you that . . . " and go on to address the *issue* and make your positive point.

Leading Question

- *Example*   "Where is all this rhetoric going to take us?"
- *Response*   Don't be led into statements you do not choose to make. Let the reporter know you understand the technique by saying, "I'm

not sure where you want to go with that, Frank, but I believe we have a solid issue here that deserves the public's support." Then go on with almost any relevant point you would prefer to make.

Multiple-Part Question

- *Example* "What's going to happen next? Will there be a recall? Do you think your competitors will follow suit? How much is all this going to cost? And can you afford it? Better yet, can the public afford it?"
- *Response* You just have been hit with six questions, and you can only answer one at a time. Simply pick the part you *want* to answer, reply to that, and let the other parts go. You are under no obligation to try to respond to every part.

Forced Choice

- *Example*. "Would you rather see the banks go under or have them return to activities that have been previously banned to them?"
- *Response* You can choose either part, both parts, or neither part of the choices the questioner offers you. It is up to you to make your *own* selection. End with a positive point.

The Loaded Question

This technique calls for more detailed discussion than the others because it is more complex to deal with.

LOADED—FALSE STATISTICS

- *Example* "Isn't it true that you cut your payroll by more than $150,000 in the last quarter, alone?"
- *Response* The trigger word is *cut*. When loaded numbers come at you, go right to the nonemotional issue contained within the question. When you do, choose your own words. *Cut* then becomes *reduced*. Correct the numbers to make them accurate. Here's how your response might sound: "On the contrary, Dick, we actually increased our payroll by some $85,000 for that quarter. We've

already made the adjustment to deal with the loss of sales you mentioned earlier, and our sales have picked up quite well."

When a question hinges on a number that is inaccurate or false, question it. Ask for the source. Ask the questioner to hold up the document. Ask him or her to hand it to you. Remain courteous. If you don't have the correct information at hand, yourself, don't try to refute it on the spot. Instead, politely say that you don't believe that the information is correct and leave yourself a way out so that you can graciously offer to get back to the interviewer with a clarification or correction.

LOADED—FAULTY LOGIC

- *Example*   "If we increase the size of the waste treatment plant, the construction of more townhouses becomes inevitable, right?"
- *Response*   This is a case of logic that leaps from fact to assumption. Simply point out facts as you know them even though your interviewer may cling to his or her assumptions.

STRIPPING LOADED QUESTIONS

Loaded questions may set you up to answer in ways that serve another's agenda. Some people who ask them intend to box you into tight corners; others ask them merely as a part of their personal style. In neither case are you obliged to allow a loaded question to victimize you. I have heard some guests respond by retaliating with, "That's a loaded question." If you follow that comment with anything like "and I'm not going to respond to it," you've again left yourself open to attack.

A better approach—one that has worked hundreds of times for my clients, even in the most stressful situations—is to listen carefully to the question, pause, and then isolate the loaded aspect. Once you've singled out the loaded words, determine the actual issue, decide how to neutralize the question, and select a way to begin your response so that you show empathy and also buy a few seconds to think.

Suppose that someone asks, "How much longer are you going to keep using the Iraq situation as an excuse for jacking up gasoline prices at the pump?" Remain calm. Put your emotional energies into the intellectual game that faces you. Ask yourself these questions:

- What are the loaded words? *Using, excuse,* and *jacking up.*
- What's at issue here? Prices.

- How can I reduce this to a neutral question? Address the issue, not the words.
- How can I begin with an empathetic statement that also gains time for me to put my thoughts in order? Start by acknowledging the questioner's intent to arouse emotions.

Here's how the answer might sound:

- Begin an opener such as, "While that's a rather strong statement, Renee. . . ."
- Then go on to say something such as, ". . . the issue here is what has caused retail gasoline prices to rise."
- Then, without hesitation, continue by saying something such as, "On that issue, we're taking into account the cost of replacing the barrels of oil that are needed to make that gasoline. The price charged for anything has to take into account the cost of replacing the product. We must be able to afford to do that so we can continue to provide the gasoline the public needs."
- Then, without pause, illustrate by adding, "For example" and conclude with an illustration that substantiates your statement.

In fewer than 100 words and in less than a minute you have reduced the loaded question, isolated the neutral issue, made a positive statement on your organization's behalf, and related this to the public interest. Further, your reply, because of its positive nature, should lead the interviewer to either ask more constructive follow-up questions or leave the answer alone. Best of all, this technique shows you can stand up under pressure without causing the other party to lose. When you exhibit this kind of poise and control, you gain everyone's respect.

Other Interviewing Devices

Reporters also employ a few other devices their guests should be aware of. Although the devices just discussed are content oriented, these are more a matter of the style in which the interviewer attempts to "make things happen."

SPEED-UP
The speed-up is a rapid-fire series of questions that leave you trying to answer one question even while others are coming at you. The inter-

viewer may be doing this unintentionally or might be trying to set a pace that irritates you and causes you to blurt out something you wish you hadn't said. To respond, answer one question at a time, and finish your response regardless of how many questions are thrown at you. To maintain your own control, slow your pace and expand your answers.

STALL

The interviewer using the stall allows you to finish answering a tough question and then remains silent, nodding his or her head up and down to cue you to say more. Although nature abhors a vacuum, don't be tempted to fill the silence by blurting out something you shouldn't say. He or she could be counting on you to do that. Here is a better way to react to the silent treatment. Say, "Does that answer your question?" or "Can I answer any other questions for you?" If the interviewer is still willing to give you empty air time, use it for "commercials": make as many positive points as you can. Eventually the interviewer will see the folly of this device.

CHORUS LINE

One, two, three—kick! If three questions that elicit simple "yes" answers come at you in rapid succession, prepare for the kick. Here's how it happens:

- *Question one* "You're pretty proud of your company's environmental record, right?"
- *Answer* "Yes."
- *Question two* "Particularly in the area of clean water, right?" (Pause.)
- *Answer* "Yes."
- *Question three* "And there's no doubt in your mind that you'd like to continue to enjoy that reputation. Am I correct?" (Pause.)
- *Answer* "Yes."
- *Kick* "Then why did we just learn that you have been discharging effluent well beyond EPA allowances into the Bruendt River for the past seven days?
- *Unprepared guest's answer* "Gulp."

How should you respond? When you say yes to two questions in a row and are given a third one, broaden your answer at once. Instead of just saying yes, keep talking. Doing so destroys the questioner's timing and the kick will never come or will at least be considerably weakened—particularly if your answer is interesting and positive.

DOUBLE WHAMMY

At one time, it was thought that "Have you stopped beating your wife?" was a clever question, but some of today's journalists have developed impressive variations on it. A question like, "You don't deny that you haven't stopped beating your wife yet, do you?" presents you with quite a dilemma. If you say no, does this mean you have stopped? Does a yes mean you haven't? Beneath it all, is either answer a good one?

Why wrestle with the problem? Treat it as a combination of a loaded, and a forced-choice question. Pause, use the interviewer's name, and address the issue. In this case, the issue is your positive relationship with your wife. Here's how it might sound: (Pause.) "Well, Phil, if I understand your question correctly, what's at issue here is my relationship with my wife. On that note, it is a fine one, indeed. Why just last week, we both happened to surprise each other by sending a dozen roses to each other's offices."

You're off the hook, leaving the interviewer either fishing for another question or commenting, "A dozen roses?"

11
Advanced Techniques for Interview Guests

A good start to any interview is to address the issue inherent in your interviewer's question in your own words, without repeating his or her language. Bridging over to the positive point you want to make is also important. However, skilled interview guests know that they must do more than that.

Brightening Your Answers

SPARKLERS
The most successful interview guests answer with a sparkler whenever possible. As I define them, sparklers are devices that add interest and color to dialogue—including relevant quotes, examples, statistics, anecdotes, similes, metaphors, and humor. These and other devices help you capture and retain the audience's interest.

Ask yourself this key question: can I come up with something brief and to the point that helps me state my case? If so, go with it. If not, you might want to work on developing this skill in your rehearsals.

TIGHT LANGUAGE
You can also brighten your answers by avoiding responses that are dull and heavy-handed. One way to improve the power of your answers is to eliminate all words that end in *sion* or *tion*. Instead of saying, "He gave an indica*tion* that the situa*tion* had been brought to a successful conclu*sion*," say this: "He said the job was done." You might say that

the elimination of "shun" words also creates a better association and retention in the minds of your viewers and listeners: in other words, "Get rid of the "shun" words and audiences are likelier to recall what you said."

To convert the "shun" words, find the working verb hidden within each word that ends with this sound. For example, *indication* contains *indicate, communication* contains *communicate,* and so on. In the video replays of your practice sessions, write down sentences that contain them, then reduce the "shun" words down to their basic components.

To practice this editing technique, have someone read the following sentences aloud so you can hear how they obscure meaning and discourage attentiveness. (These sentences were drawn from rehearsals in client seminars.)

- "Consideration of the occasion is important to ongoing relations with those who wish to make observation of this event."
- "We believe the situation will be brought to a successful conclusion."
- "The recommendation will result in an extension in the duration of our ongoing negotiations."
- "The project has reached completion as far as excavation is concerned."

Now replace the "shun" words in each statement with the root verbs. The sentences don't make much sense in this form, but they can help you focus on the kind of work each sentence needs. Here's how they look after this first pass:

- *"Consider* of the *occur* is important to ongoing *relate* with those who wish to make *observe* of this event."
- "We believe the *situate* will be brought to a successful *conclude."*
- "The *recommend* will result in an *extend* in the *endure* of our ongoing *negotiate."*
- "The project has reached the *complete* stage in as far as *excavate* is concerned."

In the next step, take the last example and tighten it up: "The project is completed as far as the excavating is concerned." With a little more paring down, this might read, "The excavating part of the project is completed." However, when a seminar participant thought about what he really needed to say, he ended up with this: "We've dug the hole."

Try this with each of the other statements, and you'll see how much more powerful they become when you strip out the "shun" words and put them to work for you. You add immediacy, action, and even drama—and all three help to keep audiences tuned in.

Passive Interviews Are Dull

People often obscure their answers by hiding behind the passive voice—a dull way to say nothing without committing yourself to even that much. Unemphatic, vague, wordy, and indirect responses fail to say who did what or who will do what. The active voice—which identifies who did what—is direct, forceful, and vigorous. It encourages brevity as well as clarity and helps you Keep It Short and Simple.

Use the active voice as much as possible, and you have a good chance to make your point clear the first time. In broadcast interviews, the audience can't refer back to something the way newspaper or magazine readers can. Listeners either stay with you or you lose them. Use the passive voice only when the action is more important than the person who does it, when you don't know who was responsible for the action, when you want to put your most emphatic point at the end of the statement, or when you wish to be diplomatic. These situations are discussed extensively in my book *How to Be Prepared to Think on Your Feet and Give the Best Business Presentation of Your Life* (New York: HarperBusiness, 1990).

Injecting Humor

Interviews are not speeches, and you should not try to tell jokes on the air. Humor is tricky enough to inject into a planned presentation; it is even more difficult to handle when you don't know what you will be asked to comment on next.

Never try to force humor in an interview; it can be awkward and embarrassing for everyone.

You should take opportunities to show your friendly and affable side. Try to have a light attitude whenever it is appropriate to do so. Don't crack one-liners or become a stand-up (or sit-down) comedian, but don't take yourself and your subject so seriously that you never smile.

CAUTIONS
Interviewers, operating in a familiar environment, may be more comfortable than you in making light remarks. This relieves you of part of the

burden, but don't allow tension to let you forget to respond to their efforts. Once rapport is lost, it is difficult to regain.

Interviews allow for a certain amount of spontaneous humor, and jokes arise out of discussion content. Be careful, however, not to participate when the so-called humor is disparaging to others. If you are uncomfortable with what you are about to say or if you think it might offend even one person, leave it out. It will make you look bad. If the joke is on you, and you brought it about, laugh. If the interviewer makes you the brunt of a joke, however, be cautious. Put-down humor, like any other, needs a response, but be certain that your attitude conveys an air of incredulity with a twinkle: convey "I can't believe you just said that" by your nonverbal reactions as you move swiftly to score the point you need to make.

HUMOR CAN HELP
When used appropriately, humor has its benefits. It can help you illustrate and underscore points that your audience might not have grasped any other way. Recall President Reagan's campaign remark in which he said of his younger opponent that he would not stoop to making youth and inexperience a campaign issue.

Humor can help you through a stressful moment, it can lighten the tone of a discussion that has become heavy, it can signal a change of pace, or it can help bring about that change. It should contribute to and compliment the flow of the dialogue and not interrupt it or call attention to itself. It should be relevant, sincere, brief, inoffensive, and fresh. It should also be used judiciously: a few, well-timed bits of humor go a long way in an interview.

HOW TO WORK IT IN
Humor should spring naturally out of the interview, but a sense of humor and an ability to use it during interviews can be acquired. Start by considering what makes *you* laugh. Collect the stories that give you a chuckle or illustrate in a lighthearted way a point that is important to you. Gather them from friends and from the publications you read. Record spontaneous bits of humor wherever you hear them if you feel you might be able to use a similar line in a future interview. As your collection grows, sort them by topic. Soon you'll have material you can use in your interviews.

The issue now becomes learning how to incorporate humor into your responses. Again, this takes practice. For starters, screen your list of positive interview points against the humorous material you have collected to see which bits might fit where. In your rehearsals, try dropping them in with the relevant responses to questions wherever they seem to fit best. In your critiques, determine which ones work, whether you are conveying them convincingly, and whether this approach is good for you to use.

On-camera rehearsals enable you to become familiar with the process, reduce stress, and increase your comfort levels. Having a positive, confident attitude during interviews helps you successfully use humor.

How Interviews Open

You have little or no control over the way your interviewer positions your appearance once the cameras begin rolling. You can influence the process somewhat, however, if you prepare what the trade sometimes calls a one-sheet—a single sheet of paper, double-spaced, that summarizes your affiliation and position on the interview topic. List your name at the top followed by the phonetic spelling—especially if the interviewer might have difficulty pronouncing it. On my one-sheet, my name is typed "Stephen (STE′-ven) C. Rafe (RAY′-fee)."

Below this, type your job title, department, organization, city, states, and phone number. Again, use phonetics where needed. Then add a brief paragraph stating the issue to be discussed in the interview and your position on it. For complex issues list three to five bulleted points in short, pithy sentences. Emphasize the positive aspects of the drama-and-conflict issues discussed in chapter 2, and answer the viewing audience's unspoken questions: "So what? Who cares? What's in it for me?"

As interview topics change, your one-sheets will also change. You should prepare a one-sheet on each topic long before you need it. Use your organization's policy statements as a starting point.

By providing the station with this information—either by sending in your one-sheet or by phone—you may influence the interviewer to select an opening favorable to your position. In fact, if you include a list of points for possible discussion, you may even guide the interviewer into asking questions that lead into the points you wish to make.

Don't provide a list of questions, however. Some interviewers resent what they see as an attempt to control the interview and may try to turn your own efforts against you. A list of points, however, serves the same purpose as questions and doesn't engender the same negative reactions.

Ultimately you have no control over whether the information you provide will be used and even less control over how questions are phrased. Don't let this concern you. You are in charge of your answers, and that's what's important.

More Advanced Techniques

As you become increasingly comfortable with being interviewed by the news media, you also will be practicing the skills presented in this book. Once you have mastered the fundamentals of news-media interviewing, you are ready for more sophisticated techniques. Minor difficult moments in your interviews often can be defused by ignoring them when they occur. Paying attention to them may give them more power than they deserve. If, however, the interview seems to be tougher than you anticipated, you have several ways to handle the situation without walking away from the cameras.

Here are the techniques I teach in my advanced communications techniques (ACT) programs.

RESPONDING TO ABUSIVENESS

You have a right—and you should exercise it—to comment directly on abusive behavior. Certainly it doesn't follow traditional protocol to do so, but if an interviewer does not treat you with respect, you should be ready to let the world know it.

The Code of Broadcast News Ethics guides some 3,500 members of the Radio-Television News Directors Association, which represents the best in the business. Item three of that code says that its members *will* (not *should*) "respect the dignity, privacy and well-being of people with whom they deal."

When you sense that you are being treated unfairly, say so. Here's a technique that one of my clients used when she was being roughed up by a grandstanding reporter. After less than three minutes she looked at him as calmly as an adult might look at an undisciplined child and said, "I would like to believe you respect your guests and would want your viewers to believe you treat them fairly. I would like that kind of treatment from you now." This powerful phrasing offers three statements of how the reporter *should* conduct himself, contains embedded commands ("respect your guests," "treat them fairly," and, in effect, "treat me that way now"), and matches nonverbal messages that direct the reporter's behavior both implicitly and explicitly. Finally, it allows the reporter to see the potential for immediate, negative consequences of his own behavior.

The reporter did knock it off, although he also terminated the interview just a few moments later, and this taped session was not used on the air. Our client would have been just as well advised to have responded this way even in a live interview, however. Such reporters represent an unprofessional and frequently inexperienced minority of those in the business, and you're not likely to meet them in the major market stations. The key to succeeding is to remain calm. Any signs of irritation or annoyance may cause such individuals to respond with more abusive behavior.

COPING WITH PERSONAL OPINIONS
Sometimes an interviewer inadvertently becomes so involved in a dialogue that he or she expresses personal views that differ from yours but without intending to attack you personally. When this happens, agree with what you can, and bridge to the point you wish to make. Here are some techniques for doing this:

- In your response, change the subject to one that is less heated.
- Find a level of dialogue on the topic that increases the comfort level for both of you.
- Turn negatives into positives by seeing things in a different light. When the rescue squad installs a new siren, it may annoy some of the neighbors but also may help save lives.
- Use another form of embedded commands by saying something such as, "You might want to consider *seeing this another way,* based on the senator's findings."
- Describe the behavior you would like to see happen in the future by saying something such as, "Once we cover what you need here, you might want to talk with the mayor about this."
- Show how your plan of action will benefit others.
- Invite the interviewer to explain his or her views more thoroughly— without having to ask a direct question. You might "wonder whether it might be a good idea to explore your point a bit further." This is somewhat like doing the forbidden—asking the interviewer questions—but doing it this way, is unlikely to arouse their ire.
- Compare whatever seems to be troubling the reporter with something else that could be worse. For instance, the plane may have crashed, but at least no one was killed.

To reduce the likelihood of resistance, preinterview negotiations become critical. Ask the people who set up your interview what they would like to talk about, and invite them to share their views on the subject with you. Once again, interviews need not have undisclosed agendas, and they don't have to catch guests by surprise to be success-ful. When understanding and rapport have been achieved beforehand, the outcome is more likely to be a successful interview for both parties.

Opposition contains within it an opportunity to explore issues and achieve understanding. It is better to have opposition out in the open— even in an interview—than to leave it unspoken where it can haunt you elsewhere. You have no need to be concerned about opposition or differences of opinion. They are opportunities for you to make construc-tive responses.

A KICKER

Another technique you can use in your responses is a variation of the interviewer's own chorus-line technique covered earlier. This time you do your own one-two-three-kick. Simply begin your response with a point that the reporter has to agree with, move to one he or she would be less likely to accept, then to a third one that might have been even less acceptable had you started off your answer with it. Follow that up with your key point. Here's how it goes:

> We all know (1) our present school system is overcrowded (pause) and that (2) our children don't deserve to be educated in trailers (pause), (3) that they are not cattle to be herded from one crowded place to another (pause). (Kick:) We need to pass this school bond issue so the children of this county receive the quality education they deserve.

Try this on any point you feel needs to be strengthened before it meets resistance, and you should encounter a high level of acceptance of your points. Like the others, this technique appears to be simple and innocent enough, and therein lies its power.

Voice Tones and Attitude

Don't reply to a hostile question or to aggressive body language with a calm demeanor and a placating voice. This response could, in fact, aggravate the questioner because of the mismatch in the attitudes and behaviors. Instead, direct your energies toward the issue, not at the questioner, and match his or her words, voice tones, and body language as closely as you can.

- *Example*   The reporter leans forward, stares at you, jabs a finger at you, and says in a demanding voice, "I want to know why your company is still bilking its customers!"
- *Response*   Lean forward, stare to one side of the reporter's face, jab your finger in the air but not *at* the reporter to punctuate each word, and say, in the same heated, staccato tones, "If *that* were the case, I would feel exactly the same way!"

Note that your words do not interpret or label the reporter's emotions. You have said that you would feel "exactly the same way," leaving the reporter to make his or her own interpretation. Keeping the topic away from the reporter's feelings helps steer the questioning away from personal debate and back to the main issues. Now go on with your statement:

- "The public has a *right* to know that their bills (or whatever) are accurate and reflect fair pricing policies." (Now ease off on the nonverbals and voice tones, and slide into your own clarification.) "In fact, (use reporter's name here), our XYZ study in 1986 did precisely that for us and showed that many customers are actually paying less on a per-unit basis than the national average."

Since follow-up questions generally stem from the content of your most recent answer, your response leads into questions about the study, the findings of the study, specific types of customers who are paying less, overall rates, or comparisons with national averages—and all were planted within your answer.

Questioning the Questioner

At times it may be appropriate, even advisable, to ask questions of your interviewer—momentarily reversing your roles. For example, you always have the right to clarify a question, particularly one that sounds accusatory of argumentative. The key to success rests within the way you ask your question. Don't deny or repeat any accusations the reporter made. Instead, keep calm, remind yourself that you want to clarify the question and determine what response the reporter seeks. Then say, "I'd like to be helpful and it would be *helpful* (intentionally repeating the word) if you would clarify your question for me." A well-intentioned reporter will clarify; a testy one may become insistent. Regardless, pick your best response and proceed.

Creating Overload

Once you are comfortable with interviews at the levels covered so far, add the overload technique. Here's how it works. You pack your answer with more bits of information, highly compressed, than the interviewer can process, which overloads the questioner with information and leaves him or her momentarily without a direction. Move quickly through the overload, and then single out what you want to call to the interviewer's attention. Do this before he or she can formulate a follow-up question.

If you have just been asked a question about an employee-reduction program, you might say,

> Well, Sarah, there are a lot of things to *consider* here. We have to *consider* the rights of the employees who have been with us longest, we have to *consider* the minority employment opportunities, the requirements we have under EEO legislation. We also have to *be sure* that the employees who remain at this particular location are going to be those employees who are competent. Administratively, we have to *be sure* that the managerial people here will be able to supervise this plant properly. We are going to *have to have* the technicians. We are going to *have to have* the specialists who know how to run the plant. But the *important* thing here, Sarah, is that we are going to have the right people to do the jobs so that this plant will continue to serve the community well after this program is in place.

Do not hesitate; do not even breathe as you run through that response. Use pacing words such as the ones we have underscored to help move your response along without interruption. Smile your best moving-right-along smile with every word. Leave no room for the questioner to interject even an "Um, hmm."

According to Miller's law of Seven, plus or minus Two, most people can deal with seven facts at a time, plus or minus two. Some people can only handle five, and others up to nine; beyond that, they are stretching toward overload. During an interview, with many questions being asked and many points being made, most interviewers have difficulty trying to deal with an answer that contains more than three bits of information. The reason has to do, in part, with mathematical permutations. If you give people one point to think about, that's all they need to be concerned with. Give them two points, and they must examine A in terms of B and B in terms of A. Give them three points to think about, and they try to consider A in terms of B and C and then in terms of C and B, in that order. They also must consider the effects of B as the prime point when related with A and C and C and A, in those orders. Finally, they have to do the same with point C in terms of B and A. This just begins the confusion. Three to the third power is nine permutations—27 different ways to think about the same facts.

When you give the interviewer four things to think about, he or she begins to reach overload. Five thoughts require juggling more than 3,000 possibilities. If you pace your points so that you are not interrupted, the interviewer is almost forced to accept the one you finally focus on.

I often use overload when conducting a studio orientation. I may say,

> Welcome to the studio. As you can see, you will have cameras pointing at you, you'll have a television monitor staring at you with your image on it, people will be clipping microphones onto your clothing, others will be moving around, there will be people holding up cards and waving their hands to give time cues. Still others may want to put makeup on you. And then someone will tell you to be comfortable. Now, how are you going to be comfortable? Well, put aside all the things I just pointed out to you. Here's how to get comfortable on television.

Participants are always eager and ready for the point that comes next— how to be successful—and that is the one I want them to hear most clearly.

All overloads must contain only information that enhances your credibility. They must consist of readily acceptable facts or points, using the rule of "seven, plus or minus two."

"Imagine with Me"

Another technique that works for sophisticated spokespersons enables you to begin your response in a way that causes the interviewer to go along with you. It requires getting the interviewer to suspend judgment momentarily. When the reporter asks you a question, here's how it might develop.

Reporter: How would you respond to charges that your company has become a liability in this community?

You: Imagine with me for just a moment, John, what would happen

if we found it necessary to leave this community. It wouldn't
be a very good story.

Automatically, you have the reporter formulating questions around
the impact of unemployment, layoffs, and so on. He or she will go along
with you because you are seemingly providing useful input for follow-up
questions, raising issues that he or she might want to pursue. However,
you aren't finished yet. Without pause, you continue:

You: But fortunately, John, that's not the story here. We intend to stay
in this community. For example, etc.

Here's another:

You: Imagine with me, if you will, what would happen to the tax base
in this community if this plant weren't still here. Think of the
effect on local business and even on this station's advertis-
ers. However, we're talking about people here, not just the
physical site—the plant that accounts for the tax revenues of more
than . . . , etc.

The reporter is imagining, indeed—especially about the loss of
advertising revenues if your company leaves. His or her next question
may be a little slow in coming, but it will most likely lead to a point you
would like to make. Wait patiently as he or she formulates the question.
The follow-up question will most likely be based on concepts suggested
by the words you used in your answer.

The "imagine" technique creates a picture in the reporter's mind,
a scenario that the reporter is likely to follow. You can open with various
phrases, such as, "Let's take a look at what would happen if" or "Let's
see if we can picture what it would be like when" or "What do you
suppose would happen if . . . ?"

Sending and Receiving Cues

Certain verbal and nonverbal tactics can give you an edge that helps you
assert your rights to make key points in a television interview.

PICKING UP TIME CUES

When the interview is down to its last minute, you will have to answer
the last question briefly. The show has to end on time. The good news

is this: you can be reasonably assured that no matter what you say, the interviewer won't have time to ask a follow-up question. Fill the time making your best point.

When the host or hostess says, "We have only a few seconds left," this is your signal to make a brief, positive statement. You will probably have about 20 seconds. Don't waste time asking for permission or explaining that you'd "just like to make a final point." Just do it.

If the interviewer doesn't give you such an obvious cue, there is still hope, and you will develop the skill with experience. In time, you should be relaxed enough during interviews to notice the floor manager giving hand signals to indicate the time remaining. Typical gestures used include raised index finger (one minute), thumb and index finger formed into the letter C (a half minute left), one index finger crossing the other at right angles (same), one arm crossing the other at right angles (same).

Some studios use cue cards to indicate the time remaining. Even if you can't see the signals, you may be able to "read" the host's acknowledgment of them. He or she may nod slightly, raise a finger, or sometimes, use just a glance to indicate that the cue has been received.

With practice, you also may develop what is known in the trade as having "a clock in your head"—a good sense of time. If you acquire this skill, and you find out beforehand how long you will be on the air, you also may determine when the time is right for you to drop in your final point.

When you pick up a time cue, no matter what question you have been asked, move to your best, positive point—fast. Be responsive, but don't waste time with preliminaries. Be brief. You may even finish your point as the credits roll—if it's interesting and you do it with the right attitude. A smile helps.

During an interview, you can assert yourself and gain the interviewer's attention with simple hand signals that let the host know, in an acceptable way, that you have a point to make. Gesture signals can be especially useful when a host rambles during a one-on-one interview. You can also use them to divert attention away from another guest whose views oppose yours.

In either case, wait until the person speaking is in the middle of a minor, or nonessential, comment—then raise your hand slightly. Just the wave of an index finger will do. Interviewers' livelihoods depend, in part, on their quickness in picking up cues that lead to interesting information or a lively show. Your hand movement also may cue the program manager to have a camera ready to cover you when the interviewer invites you to comment.

OTHER CUES

You can also cue the interviewer by moving your eyes or raising your eyebrows. A light throat clearing or cough is another way to gain attention. If you are close enough, you may touch the interviewer lightly on the arm to gain his or her attention. You must do this discreetly, however, and with a friendly face. Never reach across other guests to do this.

If you're participating in an interview with someone else from the same organization or who represents the same viewpoint, you can cue each other. A simple *Hmmm* or a single word could be your cue to one another—as long as it enables the person speaking to yield to you without interrupting or to allow you to add something at the end of the point.

No rule says you must always speak directly to the interviewer and never to a colleague. If you are speaking, you can use a cue to let your partner know you want (or need) to turn the question over to him or her. One way would be to use a name cue. For example, you could turn to him and say, "As you know, Tony, ..."

It helps if you both have worked out a simple signal beforehand, such as a key word. You have the right to do that, too.

The interviewer is likely to allow the other person to speak as long as the same train of thought is maintained—with enthusiasm. Even if the interviewer does interrupt, he or she may pursue the point, thanks to your use of names, the shirttailing on the key words, and the positive nonverbals.

Here is another way to register your point. As you deliver your key words, raise your right hand, or snap your fingers of your right hand lightly. Research shows this helps to access the right brain—the creative and imaginative side for most people. This keeps the questioner's left brain—which is the more technical or analytical side—occupied as you register your point. The gesture also helps you lock in an important thought. If you have already made the point in a positive, enthusiastic way earlier in the interview and given examples, so much the better.

One technique that is the opposite of finger snapping is the visual-verbal squash. Hold up your left hand (analytical and rational) and look at it as you speak about an idea you oppose. Next, hold up your right hand, and figuratively put an idea on it that negates the first one. To cancel out the first point, bring your hands together and squash the first idea by placing the right hand on top of the left. This puts the preferred idea in the dominant position and the other one in the subordinate or defeated position.

Asking Permission to Make a Point

Another advanced technique to use when you face reporters is called asking permission. Its value lies in its ability to allow you to ask questions of reporters—something that most people being interviewed are reluctant to do (or have been coached not to do).

- You might turn to the reporter and say, "Ted, may I give you an example of how our organization has taken care of its employees?" Reporters are not likely to say no because examples add sparkle to the interview.
- If you ask, "May I share with you what our president said recently on this issue?" you can be sure the reporter will want to know what your president said.
- If you ask, "May I tell you about the meeting we had with the mayor of the town?" the reporter will have to go along with you. If nothing else, he or she knows that the audience wants to know the answer.

This technique provides you with constructive alternatives to simply listening to questions and responding obediently. It also gives you another avenue through which you can make points that will help both the interview and your own cause.

Giving Permission to Accept the "Unacceptable"

This technique enables experienced interview guests to give the interviewer and the audience permission to think in a way that may have been contrary to their beliefs prior to the interview. It is subtle, yet it is so obvious that it may appear to be ineffective. Often, the listener doesn't realize what has transpired until the outcome has already been achieved.

It goes like this: "You know, Tom, it's okay to think about business and the public interest in the same context." This links together two concepts that the listener may have previously found incompatible. If you had said, "Tom, business operates in the public interest," you may have triggered resistance or a challenge. Instead, you have merely indicated the "okay-ness" of pairing the two within the same concept.

Since audiences retain very little of what they hear, you help to secure information in their minds when you say it's okay to think about things in a certain way. However, you should always have the facts to back up what you say. You need examples, anecdotes, or dramatic statistics to support your observations.

When you "give permission" to interviewers, you actually reduce the chances that they will pursue the issue in a hostile or challenging way. They will be more likely to ask you for the clarification that you are already prepared to provide.

Since research shows that television takes on an image of authority in the home, you benefit from that association when you "give permission." One study showed that television has more credibility than churches, police departments, and other authority figures. You capitalize on that credibility and authority when you take on a mature, confident, and reassuring stance as you respond to questions on television. You should also ensure that your voice tones reflect these characteristics.

It is much better, for example, to say in calm tones, "It's okay to think about clean air and chemicals in the same community," than it would be to say defensively, "Our chemicals have nothing to do with the air around here." The first response leaves you and the reporter with the opportunity to explore the positive benefits of having both clean air and a chemical plant in the same community.

When you "give permission" by pairing two statements in this way, you are using a powerful tool that is generally reserved for advanced, experienced interview guests. Be certain that you have your basics in place before using this technique.

Part Four
Other Types of Interviews

12
Telephone Interviews

Reporters who call to interview you by telephone know they are interrupting your immediate activities. You may be working on an important project or conducting a meeting, for example. That knowledge gives you the first tool for taking charge of the interview.

Screening Your Calls

If a secretary screens your incoming calls and says a reporter is on the line, get on the phone and say hello personally. Then tell the reporter that you are in the middle of something you need to take care of first but that you'll call them right back. If you are pressed for answers to questions, simply say that the interview is too important to rush through and you would like to give them the time they need. Don't respond to pressure. Remain calm and in control. Remember, no one can make you do anything.

Let your voice tones and your choice of words show that you welcome the opportunity to speak. Get the reporter's full name, phone number, and the name of his or her publication or station. If the reporter didn't ask you a question, ask for the issue they want to talk about. This helps you prepare yourself to provide helpful information when you return the call. You'll know which file to pull, which numbers to have at hand, and so on. Ask for the reporter's deadline, and offer to call back well within time.

This callback approach gives you the following immediate controls:

- It enables you to ensure that the caller is legitimate.
- It gives you time to gather your thoughts and notes on the issue to be discussed.
- It makes you the caller rather than the recipient of the call. Now you are in a stronger position to terminate the call when you feel the interview has run its course (but never before answering any tough questions that have just been asked of you).

By screening before you call back, you gain time to determine how important the subject is to your organization, whether you are the right person to serve as spokesperson, and, if so, how long you want to spend in an interview. It also gives you the opportunity to channel the call to a member of your staff or a senior person for policy reasons or because they can provide the reporter with better information.

When You Call Back

When you do call back—and you must do so for credibility and good-will—suggest that you have time for just one or two questions. Phone interviews that run longer should be prearranged, preceded with a discussion of the format, and conducted by mutual agreement on the ground rules. If interviewers say they need more time than one or two questions would allow, offer to schedule an interview with them in person.

Most phone interviews are brief, however, and fall into the following categories:

- *Fact check*   The reporter wants to verify information from other sources or needs additional data.
- *Round-up*   The reporter is calling you, along with others, for comments on a given issue, situation, or problem.
- *Background*   The reporter wants information on how a certain problem or process came into being.
- *Quick quote*   The reporter wants a striking statement for use in a fast-breaking story.

Before you call back, jot down your key positive points on the issue as you understand it. Have back-up information handy.

When you place your return call, assume that everything you say is being tape recorded and may be used for publication or on the air. Some reporters no longer use a beeper when taping conversations. Take your time in answering each question. You are not obliged to fill the silence, or "dead air time." Whether you are being taped or broadcast live, silence is the reporter's problem, not yours.

No matter what happens, stay courteous and cooperative. Even an apparently negative subject gives you the opportunity to tell your organization's side of the story in your own words. Be appreciative and remain calm. Stay in control of *you*. Here are some classic ways that a reporter might announce your responses on the air:

- *Cooperative* "A (your organization) spokesperson said today, 'The economy is still rough, and the company has put some 300 employees on alternate work weeks to preserve their jobs.' The spokesperson said the plant does not foresee a turnaround in the near future but does not anticipate any actual layoffs."
- *Avoiding or evading* "Repeated calls to (your organization) to ask about layoffs were not returned. This may mean that the problem at (your organization) is serious, but the company is ducking the issue."
- *Refusal to comment* "At (your organization), a company spokesperson would only say, and I quote: 'We have no comment on that issue.' This leaves us to draw our own conclusions from that one."
- *Not for attribution* "While declining to have himself or his company identified, one local plant manager said production has dropped off critically in the current recession and layoffs are inevitable. He refused to be identified, he said, because he did not want local employees to be concerned."

Additional Tips for Telephone Interviews

In the absence of being able to see your body language, people on the other end of the line—including those who hear your responses on radio and television—need your voice to hold their interest. If you want the audience to respond well to your comments, keep your voice interesting. You will need all the tools we discussed earlier, especially variety, rate, tone, and inflection. You also should be brief. In a taped interview, a dull, flat, and long-winded response might not be used on the air, but if it is used, the audience will assume that it reflects your organization's personality ("That's the kind of people they have there") or that you reflect your organization's attitude toward the issue.

Telephone (and radio) interviews rely on the auditory sense, yet most people use visual as their primary tool for accessing information, auditory as their second, and kinesthetic as their third. To establish rapport, you should use language that appeals to their visual mode first, but then to give listeners a "clearer picture" you should include both auditory and kinesthetic verbs—with more emphasis on the auditory since you are talking to listeners.

Be sure to gesture as you speak because gestures add animation to voice. Do not cradle the phone on your shoulder: this creates a tension point and makes you sound stressful. Don't doodle. This is a distracting activity that will divert energy from the enthusiasm your voice needs.

Do your best to speak in a well-modulated voice and at a moderate rate. Listeners respond better to a moderate rate than they do to a voice that is either too rapid or too slow.

Don't interrupt. This comes across even worse on the phone or on radio than it does in person. If you don't know whether a caller is finished speaking, wait four seconds before you speak.

Finally, regard all phone calls from the news media as invitations to have your organization's side of a story told accurately and positively to the audiences they reach. With proper preparation, you will be able to turn every media call into an opportunity.

13
News Conferences

P ublic relations professionals determine when and why to hold news conferences. I am ambivalent, at best, about the value of news conferences and have come to believe that few situations can replace one-on-one communication.

In fact, in the one case where a news conference might have been justified in my career, I elected to position it as a news briefing, instead. I was in charge of media relations for Texaco in New York when Ed Cole of General Motors announced that the oil industry had to remove the lead from gasoline in order for Detroit to make clean-burning automobiles. I also was involved with the task force that led Texaco to become the first U.S. company to respond to that specific challenge. (Amoco had a lead-free gasoline before that challenge was made.) The task force announcement took place in Los Angeles, where environmental concerns were being expressed with particular enthusiasm at that time.

Our specific challenge, as we saw it, was to tell the press we were *taking something out of a product and charging more for it.* The news conference format would have had the media anticipating announcements and pronouncements. Instead, with the help of Texaco's public relations person in California, we anticipated what the media wanted and expected to hear and then delivered both the content and the company executives who could conduct the thorough briefing we needed. Although the event certainly could have become a soapbox for many other hot industry issues, positioning it as a briefing enabled us to focus on the topic of lead-free Texaco gasoline, and the media were supportive of the company's efforts.

Establish the Rules

In a news conference or briefing, you need to work to maintain control even though this event takes place on your time and on the turf you have chosen. Crowd management is a primary concern. Decide on your rules beforehand, announce them at the outset, and then stick to them. This is fair to all. If you bend for even one person, you risk losing control entirely. Should that happen, call a time out until everyone settles down. Simply stand fast, and don't continue until you're ready. Reporters have to play by your rules if they want their questions answered. Be careful, though. Act unreasonably, and they'll get their story elsewhere.

Among your controls, make certain you insist on seeing the credentials of every reporter who enters the room. This may not give you 100 percent assurance that all participants are legitimate members of the fourth estate, but it helps to screen out those who might use *your* forum to grandstand for *their* issues.

If governmental or other organizations are involved in the issue, consider carefully whether you want to share your podium with them. Usually you have better control if only your own people present information.

Although this book's focus is on spokesperson skills rather than the details of staging special events such as news conferences, anyone who holds such an event is well advised to check power capacities, have people on hand to handle crowd control, and have a contingency plan for things that might go wrong.

Teleconferences

If there is more than one camera at the originating location of a teleconference, the director most likely will have one camera cover the questioners, put at least one on you, and possibly use another for reaction shots and additional angles.

ON-SITE QUESTIONING

Look directly at the reporter asking a question until he or she is finished speaking, and continue looking at the questioner as you begin your response. Only then is it permissible to share your eye contact with others. The camera that covers you should show you being attentive at all times, and your eye contact conveys that. Viewers at your other locations depend entirely on their video screens in assessing your courtesy, sincerity, and other attributes. Your attentiveness is the only measure they have. Be especially attentive when you are being asked a difficult question. A close shot of you looking up, down, or away conveys an uncomplimentary image.

If the crew is in your employ, have the director use medium shots while you listen to the question and when you first begin to respond, so that if you inadvertently break eye contact, the situation is not magnified as it would be with an extreme closeup of your face and eyes on the screens.

Once you begin responding to the question, the director can be more flexible in using closeups of you—perhaps by intercutting with shots of the questioner or others in the audience. In covering the audience, the director should generally not hold a shot too long on one person because his or her nonessential movements can become distracting. The director also should select only those audience members whose eye contact communicates that they are being attentive.

REMOTE QUESTIONING

Before the conference, ask the director which camera will be on you when a question comes from one of your remote locations. You usually can check this by observing which camera has a red light on. Look at the right camera as the questioner is speaking and continue looking at it as you begin your response. The questioner does not see you in person: you come to him or her only as a two-dimensional image on a television screen. Moreover, questioners often seek the reassurance, through your nonverbal communication, that you are listening. This is especially true when they are asking a question of a person in another city. In a phone conversation, you expect periodic feedback, such as, "I see," "Hummm," and "Uh huh," or you begin to wonder whether the other person is listening. A teleconference caller or questioner needs this reassurance and will feel that you are not properly attentive if you don't look directly at the camera. Incidentally, when the picture on the screen appears as though you are looking at the questioner, *all* viewers feel that you are looking directly at them.

The technique of looking directly into the camera is also effective when you are doing an interview in one studio and the questioner is at another location. Although you have no one with whom to establish and maintain eye contact, creating the illusion that you are in eye contact during your interview is one of the easiest ways to help ensure the success of your appearance on the program.

Once again, look at the person who is speaking or the person to whom you are speaking. When the moderator is making announcements or inviting questions, you will be seen as giving him or her your undivided attention should the director put a shot of you on screen. Maintain this eye contact, even if you happen to be reaching for a sip of water between responses. Eye contact during teleconferences is especially important when one of your colleagues is fielding a question because the audience is more likely to regard his or her comments as being important.

TURNING OVER QUESTIONS

If you receive a question during a teleconference (or a panel discussion on which you appear with a colleague) that you want to turn over to your colleague for a response, announce your intention to do so first, finish your sentence, and then look to the colleague as you finish. This gives the other person time to collect his or her thoughts. It also gives the director time to widen the shot to encompass both of you, set a camera on the colleague, and make a smooth transition. Further, it shows you as being courteous to the colleague well beyond the courtesy of your early warning.

Here is a point I have found necessary to emphasize with several clients, including one that we coached for a highly successful national news teleconference. All participants sitting on the dais may have questions turned over to them at any time and should keep their minds tuned in to the person speaking. In a teleconference, everyone in front of the cameras should look at the speaker and look interested even if they've heard the answer a hundred times, otherwise the audience will be less likely to give proper value to what is being said. Even worse is to have your thoughts wandering and then suddenly hear the speaker use your name and ask you to respond to a question or point you did not even hear. Eye contact is an important way to block out distractions and keep thoughts focused on the topic being discussed.

14
Ambush and Crisis Situations

If you suddenly find yourself being ambushed by reporters, remain pleasant. Say that you will be pleased to accept questions (if you are willing to do so) but that you were not expecting an interview and would like a moment to collect your thoughts. On the other hand, if you are not prepared to comment at the moment but would be willing to do so later, say that you will be pleased to meet with them and that they should call you for an appointment because you need to leave now. (Important tip: Studies have shown that people will permit all forms of behavior when the word *because* precedes it. In one test, when a person cut in front of a long line at the copy machine and said politely, "Excuse me, please, because I have to make copies," the people in line allowed the individual to go ahead an overwhelming number of times.)

CATCH YOUR BREATH

If you choose to proceed with the interview, introduce yourself to the reporters and try to shake their hands. This catches them off stride, which they may not like very much. Certainly, it is an unexpected action—but so is their presence.

Ambush interviewers rely on the element of the unpredictable, and you can, too. Yes, they are in a hurry to get their stories, and they may have deadlines. These are not your concern: you are not beholden to their requirements or obliged to meet their employers' needs. If they want your responses, they need to cooperate with you.

As you catch your breath, formulate the one or two key points you might want to make during this opportunity. Tell them you that you only have X amount of time for questions, and then acknowledge the least aggressive reporter in the group.

DETERMINING THE ISSUE

There is a good chance that you know the topic they are covering. If not, perhaps the first question they fire at you as they pop into view will give you some clues.

In any case, listen carefully to the question you just invited. Other reporters may try to break in, so establish strong eye contact with the reporter with whom you're speaking and ignore the others as you complete your response. Again, remain calm and courteous—even when they don't.

ESTABLISH YOUR OWN PACE AND SPACE

If you need to slow the pace, ask each reporter's name and media affiliation as you take his or her questions. You have the right to this information. Keep in mind the techniques covered in this book, and use them.

Crowding can be a problem for many people. It is human nature to want to defend one's space, and some people react more strongly than others when their territory is invaded. Ambush reporters, however, in their sometimes frenzied effort to get their microphones closer than others and get their questions asked, have been known to nearly trample the person they were trying to interview.

Hold your ground. Don't let them crowd you, but avoid commenting about the closeness of the mikes. If you feel closed in, use broad gestures: reporters will pull back if you whack their microphones with the back of your hand as you gesture and speak.

Complete the answers to the questions you accept. Don't accept questions from people you haven't acknowledged—unless you happen to hear one you like better than the one you're answering. The same holds true for interruptions. Push through to your answers unless you prefer to answer the question that interrupts you.

Ambush reporters have their own agenda. Try to help them achieve it to the extent you can do so without compromising yourself in any way. You know your rights. I've spelled them out earlier in this book. Just be sure to assert them when you are in an ambush situation.

When a Crisis Strikes

Any organization should plan for all possible crisis contingencies. Although this book's purpose is not to outline such plans, the following actions will help you succeed as a spokesperson should a crisis occur:

- *News statement*   Prepare an initial news statement that covers time and place of the crisis and numbers of persons involved. It should describe the nature of the crisis but not the cause, since that will have to be investigated, or the dollar value of property damage.
- *Initial briefing*   Read from your prepared statement in your initial briefing. Handle speculative questions in the ways covered previously: keep the door open to get back to reporters with more details or to respond to any further questions they may have as the story develops. Again, you want them to come to you for their information.
- *Remain the source*   Let the news media know you appreciate the opportunity to help them get the story told quickly, completely, and accurately and that it's in your best interest, as well as theirs, to work together. You want to remain the source.
- *Security*   If the news media cannot be admitted to the emergency area for safety or security reasons, let each reporter know this. Then offer to allow the media to interview a company employee who can serve as eyewitness.
- *Keep your promise*   If you make a promise, keep it.

In crisis situations, reporters sometimes use another questioning technique not found in other kinds of interviews. I call it the justification query, and it may be phrased like this: "How could you possibly have allowed this to happen?" This goes beyond a straight, facts-eliciting question such as "What was the cause?" and to the uninitiated spokesperson often implies guilt or blame. Again, attitude is everything. Simply regard this kind of query as a speculative or conjectural question rather than a threatening or accusatory one, and proceed from there.

If follow-up interviews are needed, keep these points in mind:

- Have only one spokesperson for all contacts with the news media.
- Have a way out of any briefing should it begin to run too long.
- If a question puts you in a negative light, acknowledge the point, and then tell how you're correcting the situation.
- Listen to the whole question before you respond.
- Follow all the guidance offered in previous chapters for dealing with reporters and their techniques.

15
Other Opportunities

You can tell your story, or have a story told about you, on radio and television in many other interview formats—on panel discussions, in responses to negative news items and editorials, in video productions, and in editorial board briefings.

Panel Discussions

A panel discussion can be a fairly low-key talk show or an aggressive, confrontational interview that includes controversial guests whose viewpoints oppose your own. Hosts of panel programs do more homework than hosts of programs that have other formats, in part because they manage and balance everyone's on-air time.

In nearly all panel discussions questions are specific and related to the topic at hand.

Your hosts may be working from a list of questions that they or their researchers have developed from information provided by guests and others. With practice and experience, once you know the issue and the thrust of the program, you can anticipate their questions and make your main points in response.

Even in friendly interviews the questioner takes an adversarial role at times. The host usually listens attentively to the guests' responses to the questions, the format and the time allotted may allow little opportunity for them to ask follow-up questions based on the content of their guests' answers. Thus, if there is more than one interviewer or two or more guests, your responses have to be brief, concise, and clear to the audience at home. You will have little or no opportunity to amplify or clarify, so keep in mind the positive point or two you want to work into the interview, and exercise whatever opportunities may be given to you to include those positive points in your responses.

Since you may have only two or three opportunities to respond to questions in a panel interview, the words you choose must be right. Time is limited. Be concise. Support your position with facts. Use anecdotes or actual cases to emphasize your points and help the audience to relate to them.

Research the positions and attitudes of your co-panelists so that you can anticipate their points. If those points conflict with yours, don't become defensive; instead, be prepared to express and support your views.

Even in programs that are conducted in a courteous manner, guests may interrupt each other or interviewers may interrupt guests who give long-winded or boring responses. When this happens, the interviewer may shift to another aspect of the topic at hand or, on occasion, to another topic in a related area.

You might be given an opportunity to make your positive point briefly near the beginning of the segment when the host or hostess turns to you for an opening comment. Be ready with well-organized, concise remarks you can interject to make a positive statement. If there are two or more guests on the show, however, you may have to stay alert to strategic opportunities to insert a positive point after the opening.

SHIRT-TAILING

One proven technique for getting your statement heard in a panel discussion is to shirt-tail right on the end of another guest's response, just as though you were merely finishing his or her sentence. Listen for a key word or phrase in the guest's answer, and as soon as he or she pauses, pick up that word or phrase, precede it with *and*, and continue from there. For instance, if the guest says, "in genetic research today," you add without missing a beat, "and genetic research is something" continuing to make your positive point.

In fact, once you begin this technique, you must push right on through a minor interruption to get to your point. The key is to be brief. If the interviewer stops you, however, break off immediately.

LOOKING RELAXED

You can appear more relaxed by leaning slightly toward the interviewer whenever he or she is speaking. Convey the feeling of being interested in what is taking place or being involved even when you are not speaking.

Look at other speakers, even if they are not looking at you and especially if the person speaking is a colleague or another person who supports your organization's viewpoint.

Avoid nodding your head up and down in an agreement gesture when the speaker says something that opposes your views.

MAKING POINTS

If you feel it is essential to make your point—when a critic is cutting your position to ribbons, for example—you may need to attract the host's attention. Do so with decorum, by reaching forward with an open hand or gesturing slightly with a pencil or pen. This will catch the interviewer's eye, raise the possibility of interesting repartee, and probably provide you with the opportunity to speak. The host may not let you interrupt your critic to get your point in, but the gesture almost guarantees that you will be called on for rebuttal. Good news reporters look for conflict and drama to keep the audience tuned in.

If you get the floor in this manner, be sure not to debate. Instead, crisply score your positive point and then relinquish the floor to the host or hostess.

This technique can be used just once in an interview, so use it judiciously. Pick your best time.

Responding to Negative News Items

If a radio or television station has made inaccurate statements about you, your organization, or its products or services, you may feel that a rebuttal is in order. Don't react too quickly, however. Left unacknowledged, most audiences will forget this editorial after a week since viewers only recall about 10 percent of what they've seen on television a week later. Responding to negative charges is a risky business because almost every rebuttal is prefaced by the original charges, which brings them to the attention of people who did not hear them the first time and reinforces them among people who heard the statements you plan to refute. The bad news about this is that words that are repeated are best remembered. Repetition aids reinforcement. The more frequently the audience hears these negatively charged words, the more likely they will recall and believe them.

A HYPOTHETICAL CASE

Say the six o'clock news has just carried a negative item about your company's products. In its broadcast, the reporter stated that your company refused to recall your electronic Baby-Tenders (a fictitious product)—a device that monitors the baby's activity from another room and provides a relaxing heartbeat sound.

You immediately prepare a news statement that states these facts: the model III in this line has caused minimal shock in three instances in which the wire to the nine-volt battery protruded from the case and contacted a metal clip that holds the device in place. You are preparing to recall this line but keep the other lines on the market.

You carry this statement to the station and after some conversation feel assured that the station will correct its previous story on the next evening's broadcast.

The correction is read over the air, yet, despite your best efforts, here's how it comes out:

> In yesterday's broadcast, we said the Semper Company was refusing to recall *all* of its electronic Baby-Tenders because they can *cause a severe shock* when in contact with moisture in *babies'* cribs and playpens.
>
>   The company has advised us, however, that most of their Baby-Tender line does not *cause shock* and that the *shock* from the model III is minimal and has only *affected three babies.* The company says it is willing to recall *only* this model of the product and is awaiting comments from the Consumer Products Safety Commission *before* doing so.

What have you gained? At best, you have gotten your correction. At worst, you have caused all the negatives—even in the correction—to be repeated, called attention to the story for the first time among those who missed it the night before, and repeated it for those who heard the story when it was first run. Further, right or wrong, a denial leads certain segments of any audience to conclude that there must be something to the charges: "where there's smoke, there must be fire."

WHAT TO DO

If you feel you must respond to a news item despite the potential negatives, ask the station not to repeat the negative charges in setting up your response. Show them the text of your response and offer to read it on the air or ask them to do so. Try to keep it to 60 seconds or less and use only positive words.

Editorial Rebuttals

When the news media editorialize and offer their opinions rather than simply report, you are facing formidable opposition. If you are granted your request for equal time (which the station is under no legal obligation to provide), you will have to work hard to increase your chances for success.

WRITING THE REBUTTAL
Here is the sequence I recommend to my clients:

1. Ask for a printed text of the editorial statement.
2. Scan the printed text, and circle all the points it makes.
3. Review the text, and underscore the points to which you want to respond.
4. Go back again, and underscore those points to which you do *not* want to respond.
5. Ask yourself why you do or do not want to respond to any points you have underscored. Are the charges false or inaccurate? Are the charges true and unable to be denied?
6. Do not use the opportunity to issue an editorial reply to repeat any negative charges or misstatements in your own wording: the media do not follow the rules of formal debate. Your response should include only positive statements.
7. Consider additional points you can make to strengthen your case.
8. Make a laundry list of all the points you want to include in your editorial reply.
9. Include no more than three positive points in your reply.
10. Jot down the main point or theme of your reply.
11. Decide how you want to end. Generally, you are most effective when you help the listening audience know why your words are right and how your views have value and meaning to them.
12. From your laundry list of facts, jot down those that best lead into your ending. Use an index card for your notes.
13. Arrange those points in a logical sequence—generally from most acceptable to least so you build from strong agreement.

14. Supplement these notes with additional relevant facts.
15. Decide how you want to begin. Don't begin by repeating the negative charges.
16. Add relevant facts to your beginning.
17. Review your laundry list one more time. Is there anything you want to include? If so, decide whether it should be in the ending, middle, or beginning, and include it accordingly. Reject the rest.
18. Be sure you have at least one key supporting point in the end, the middle, and the beginning.
19. Be sure the sequence leads the audience to your conclusion.
20. Recheck your opening statement. This is your headline.
21. Clear your intended remarks with your law department and public relations department.
22. Read your statement aloud to be sure it flows smoothly.
23. Think about your attitude. You should be pleased to have the opportunity to speak. Strive for a tone that communicates "We're all in this together."
24. Remember that the audience wants to know why they should care. In effect, they ask, "What's in it for me?"

A CASE IN POINT

Since any rebuttal may reinforce the information you are refuting or present it to people who may not have heard the original charges, make the most positive statement you can, and only indirectly address the charges that triggered your rebuttal. This is a complex task and provides the opportunity to underscore points made elsewhere or to bring new information to light that can apply in other interview situations.

Let's consider a case that is based on a client's actual experience. Here we have changed the station's call letters, the union's name, the company's name, and certain proprietary details.

EDITORIAL

WASQ-TV believes it is time for the American Pencil Manufacturers Union to organize Leadpoint's workers to come to a head.

For months, we've been hearing APMU claims that the majority of Leadpoint's employees want the union. But so far, we haven't seen any representative elections at the plants to settle the issue.

WASQ-TV suggests that the National Labor Relations Board schedule simultaneous elections at eastern and western Leadpoint plants as soon as possible.

APMU claims that Leadpoint pays the lowest wages while charging top dollar for its products. The union also claims that Leadpoint has been exposing employees to potentially toxic dust without giving them a full understanding of the danger.

Months ago, a Leadpoint vice president stated that there was no conclusive evidence that the Occupational Safety and Health Administration has significantly reduced accident and illness rates in the workplace. Leadpoint excludes union personnel from its plant safety committee.

Perhaps the APMU can remedy this if they win, or perhaps the threat of unionization, alone, will be enough to cause Leadpoint to shape up.

This is "Viewpoint," and that's the editorial opinion of the management of WASQ-TV.

Consider the Elements   Examine the text carefully, and isolate the key elements. At this point, make no judgments about right or wrong. Just list the points in the order in which the station carried them:

- American Pencil Manufacturers Union
- Organize Leadpoint's workers
- APMU claims majority of Leadpoint's employees want the union
- Haven't seen any representative elections
- National Labor Relations Board to schedule simultaneous elections
- Eastern and western Leadpoint plants
- As soon as possible
- APMU claims that Leadpoint pays the lowest wages
- Charging top dollar for its products
- Union also claims Leadpoint has been exposing employees to potentially toxic dust without giving them a full understanding of the danger
- Leadpoint vice president stated that there was no conclusive evidence that the Occupational Safety and Health Administration has significantly reduced accident and illness rates in the workplace
- Leadpoint excludes union personnel from its plant safety committee
- Perhaps APMU can remedy this if it wins
- Perhaps the threat of unionization will cause Leadpoint to shape up

Your Next Step   Now review the piece one more time and circle all speculative, conjectural statements, irrelevant statements, and inaccurate statements.

Developing Your Points   Reach back into your file of positive points, and pull those that may be relevant, even if they seem somewhat remote at first. (Remember bridging.) Here is the random list of issues to address that our client initially selected for possible use:

- Spiraling cost of living and inflation
- Leadpoint is a key employer in the area
- Unions are not necessary; no proof of value
- Wages are competitive or higher
- Product prices are fair, reasonable
- Health and safety record excellent; support with statistics, awards
- Union sits on policy-making committee
- Employees say cost of unions outweighs benefits
- Survey shows most employees reject union

Roughed-out Response   Here is a first pass at trying to put these thoughts in a sequence that best serves their needs:

> Leadpoint is a key employer in this area, offering wages that are higher than the average for this area, according to a recent, statewide survey conducted by the Bureau of Business Practices.
>
> We are proud of our excellent health and safety record. This plant has won national awards and recognition for the standards it has established. Health and safety are important here for two reasons: a plant that has healthy and safe employees is an economic and efficient operation, and even more important, all of us who work here care about one another.
>
> That caring is reflected even at the highest, policymaking, levels of Leadpoint, where a national union representative participates in every decision that concerns the health and safety of our employees.
>
> Our employees tell us there is no evidence that being represented by a union will give them anything more than they already enjoy. In fact, a recent study indicated that they believe that representation would cost them more than they would receive in return.
>
> We're inclined to listen to our our employees and respect their wishes. This is how Leadpoint has always operated and will continue to operate— with our employees' best interests in mind.

Final Edits   The piece went through two more edits and was used on the air. Our client has asked that we not print the final draft here because the company feels that doing so would readily identify it and could reveal more of its strategy than it wishes to make public. As always, we respect our clients' wishes to keep information proprietary.

We can say, though, that the piece that aired was presented from the employees' perspective entirely and incorporated some of the advanced techniques found in this book. Leadpoint attributes its success to sound labor-management practices and regards its position statements as a reflection of its policies.

When You Become the Talent

At some point during your career you may be asked to go on camera not as a guest for an interview and not as a spokesperson for a news conference but as the talent for a video production. It may be live, but more likely it will be taped. You may be asked to provide new-employee orientations, training messages, safety information, tours of new facilities, briefings of employees at remote locations, greetings for meetings and conferences, and even public service announcements on behalf of outside, charitable organizations.

In fact, many large organizations have videotaping capability today, and some have studios that are even better than those found at many commercial television stations. Those who run these facilities have told me for more than a decade that one problem persists: the people who appear on the tapes are often totally unprepared for the experience. "How can we turn them from executives into actors just long enough to have them put some oomph into their appearances without losing their personalities in the process?" one studio manager asked me. He reflected a concern expressed by many.

Executives who are comfortable in environments with which they are familiar become markedly uncomfortable when they enter an environment this foreign for the first time. If they have good experiences in media situations, they do increasingly better; if they have bad experiences, they are not likely to want to try again. Regrettably, too many bad experiences take place.

This need not happen to you. In fact, you already have increased your chances of having a positive experience before the camera just by reading this book. You have a clear idea of what to expect.

In this format you have to do many of the things done by interview hosts. You may have to use a TelePrompTer, take cues from the floor manager, and work to convey your personality.

BACK TO BASICS

Starting with what you know and can do well always provides a good foundation for acquiring additional skills in a new setting. You already know the importance of expressing your convictions, keeping eye contact, using effective body language, speaking through the camera to your audience, and using your voice in an interesting manner. In this setting, you have the advantage of working from cue cards or from a script on a TelePrompTer. Other than that, the only thing left to learn is the relatively easy skill of moving about on cue.

TELEPROMPTER

Many executives resist using a TelePrompTer. For executives accustomed to having hard copy in their hands, the greatest fear seems to be that they will be unable to see the words clearly from the required distance or that the lines of text will not be fed at a comfortable speed.

Adapting to the TelePrompTer is much easier when you have delivered presentations by using overhead transparencies or slides as your cue cards because you are less dependent on having a printed script in front of you. A prompter is an effective tool for delivering your videotaped messages while maintaining that all-important eye contact with viewing audiences—eye contact that enhances your sincerity and credibility. Looking down at script or notes on camera—particularly in close-up shots—makes some viewers uncomfortable because they see only your forehead and what appear to be half-closed eyes.

The Typescript   Using a TelePrompTer begins with entering a typescript into a computer or feeding sheets through a conveyor that has a camera positioned above the pages. The rate at which the copy is fed is a major concern to most presenters, but you, and you alone, determine the rate. The average delivery rate is about 150 words per minute, but operators are trained to follow your pace and are prepared to adjust the speed—line by line—so you can proceed comfortably. Since three or more lines are visible on the prompter at all times, operators have ample time to make ongoing adjustments. If you doubt this, try speeding up and slowing down during your delivery in rehearsal, and you will see that you set the operator's pace, not the other way around. After you've tested this, make sure you tell the operator you were merely experimenting and will not display the same fluctuations during your actual delivery and taping.

Where the Words Appear   The copy is almost always transmitted to the front of the camera or cameras you will be using. The prompter copy is superimposed on a clear screen in front of the camera's lens: you can see it clearly as you look into the camera, but the camera will not pick up and transmit the word images. Some prompters display copy from a monitor onto sheets of clear plastic that are mounted on stands, but you are unlikely to use this type during videotaped presentations.

If you are not using a computer-generated system, you can have your script typed in any readable typeface, according to the line widths your prompter system is prepared to handle. Some can display more characters horizontally than others. If you have the option, type no more than 34 characters per line, and use a large speech typeface with upper- and lowercase letters. If the equipment allows, set up the lines in whole phrases, using 1½ line spacing, and do not try to justify the right margins.

It can be disconcerting to try to read from equipment that gives you only about three or four words per line. Perhaps it's called a prompter because it works best when you are familiar with your script (see box).

The key to success here is to know your material before you go on camera and then practice delivering it from the prompter. Some people are naturals at prompter delivery, but don't count on your ability to do a cold reading. Allow ample rehearsal time with the prompter.

ON-CAMERA TECHNIQUES

As you read from prompters and stare into cameras, an audience is watching you. You have to work even harder to be animated and enthusiastic than you do during media interviews or before live audiences.

One way to help yourself maintain enthusiasm is to deliver your messages to the operators on the other side of the cameras rather than directly to the hardware. If this technique doesn't work well for you at first, ask an associate to stand very close to the camera and give you strong, positive nonverbal feedback. These listening cues will help give you the feeling of a real audience.

Where two or more cameras are used, each should have its own prompter. Someone, usually the floor manager, will cue you as to which camera you should look into. Multiple cameras add visual variety, but

---

Here's how a segment of your script might look on a prompter that can display only a few words per line:

> from the first effort
> we have seen a growing
> increase in support at
> all levels.

rehearse thoroughly with just one camera before you try to take on a multiple-camera situation—even in rehearsal. Patience and practice are the bywords to successful use of TelePrompTers.

Producing Video and Audio Tapes

A thorough discussion of the costs and techniques of video production is beyond the scope of this book, but the flexibility of the medium allows various levels of quality and expense according to how the tapes will be used. You should compare these levels with the appropriateness of sending a photocopied memo under some circumstances and a four-color brochure under certain others. Your communications professionals can offer guidance on this. People are accustomed to receiving most of their information from this medium, and tapes can be a valuable tool in your information program. Videodisks are especially effective for training needs because their computerized flexibility provides a useful self-instructional tool.

Don't overlook opportunities to make audiotapes of your messages, as well. They are economical and very effective when you develop your script and then deliver it according to the guidelines for telephone interviews (see chapter 12).

SCRIPTS
The audience's unspoken questions—"So what? Who cares? What's in this for me?"—are just as important here as they are in your news-media interviews. They should be addressed right along with "who, what, when, where, and why?"

If you want your messages to be received, understood, accepted, and acted on, you should not let too many people tamper with your script. Find a good writer, and agree to accept his or her judgment on what works and what doesn't. Crusade, if you must, against copy consensus by committee. My book *How to Be Prepared to Think on Your Feet and Give the Best Business Presentations of Your Life* (New York: HarperBusiness, 1990) provides sound advice on targeting audiences and preparing scripts. You may want to refer to it when you prepare scripts for audio and video delivery.

USING SCRIPTWRITERS
Video and audio scripts differ from speeches. It takes a special talent to write a script that works and a patient professional to remain unruffled

through the bureaucratic process to which scripts often are subjected. Respect these professionals, and value their talents highly. Many tend to be less assertive than they have a right to be. Give them all the information they need—including the opportunity to discuss each project personally with you. Reward them well, and respect the integrity of the product you've paid them to develop for you.

Once the project is under way, you may have to merge the script with the scenes and actions that will take place on camera. Depending on the scope of your project, you may find yourself blocking out days and even weeks to get the job done right. Once you begin a production, it takes on a life of its own. Contract only for what you are willing and able to commit to, and then make sure you deliver. The project depends on you. You won't spend much time producing a tape that requires you to read enthusiastically from a prompter on a single-camera shoot and that uses visuals that are character-generated on screen. Including several locations, several camera angles, music tracks, and more, however, is a major production—even if it is done economically. (In this business, as in many others, it is better to do less and do it well than it is to try to do too much and end up doing it poorly.)

Editorial Board Briefings

Editorial boards of newspapers and magazines present an excellent opportunity to communicate with executives to understand their editorial viewpoint. Their slant on the news determines what they select to print and how they report these stories. Their actual opinions on issues should be expressed only on the editorial pages, but editorial columnists' pieces are sometimes more influential than the board's editorial statements.

BOARD RESPONSIBILITIES
At large papers editorial boards meet formally and include the publisher, executive editor, managing editor, senior editors, and editor of the editorial page. Frequently editorial columnists as well as special section editors are included when the issue involves their area of editorial coverage.

The board generally examines ongoing and developing issues as well as new issues. Board members try to learn as much as possible from each other about these issues and frequently research them before taking a position and developing an editorial position.

MEETING WITH THE BOARD

If your organization's activities occur in the territory these newspapers cover, meet with their editorial boards. They will be receptive and accessible to proposals to talk with your key executives. If the issue is important enough and you have something significant to say on that issue, you should be able to get a hearing with the editorial boards of the newspapers that are affected—especially if the developing or emerging issue is controversial and affects their readers.

This is not an opportunity to make a sales pitch. Your presentation must be reasoned and supported with facts. Because most journalists tend to teeter somewhere between the passive aspects of approach and avoidance personalities (discussed in chapter 4), you should approach them in a way that fulfills their needs and expectations of you.

How to set up such briefings lies beyond the scope of this book, but you should follow all the advice provided in this book during your editorial board meetings. In addition, you may also want to review my book *How to Be Prepared to Think on Your Feet and Give the Best Business Presentation of Your Life* (New York: HarperBusiness, 1990) for its advice on preparing and delivering presentations.

The meeting generally goes something like this: you meet everyone, briefly exchange small talk, and then make a presentation that should last not more than 25 minutes. Keep the amount of talking *at* them as short as possible so that you have more time to talk *with* them through questions and discussion. Because you have even more right to ask questions in this format than in any other, be prepared to elicit their views and not just expound on your own. The entire session lasts about an hour in most cases.

YOUR FORMAT

Plan to go as a team consisting of as many as three executives, including the CEO, the financial officer, and the person who is responsible for the issue on a day-to-day basis within your organization. Keep your visuals simple and to the point. Content outweighs expensive graphics that say nothing.

Your CEO should open and introduce the other presenters and then provide an executive summary that lists your key points. Then the issues person should speak, followed by your financial officer, if appropriate, who discusses the economic aspects of the issue. The CEO concludes the presentation.

More than in any other setting in which you deal directly with the news media, you have the opportunity to "tell" people what to do. You probably will create resistance, however, if you do that directly. Keep in mind the personality types you are likely to be dealing with, and call their attention to their role in terms of the issue and their ability to affect. You can suggest actions they might want to take on their readers' behalf, but this is about as far as you should go to try to influence any subsequent actions they might take.

Conclude in a professional way, thank board members for their time, and leave. When the meeting is over, it's over. Follow through as you would with any meeting, by sending an appropriately worded letter to the person who coordinated and scheduled your meeting for the newspaper and asking that he or she extend your appreciation to the others. You can summarize your points briefly in this letter, but avoid making a sales pitch. Your goal is to keep the dialogue open.

Epilogue

I believe—and can demonstrate—that we are in control of our relationships with interviewers and that there are as many opportunities for good interviews as there are for negative ones. In my view, it comes down to this: those who make bad decisions, misunderstand the news-gathering process, or prepare poorly for interviews tend to have more negative experiences with the news media than those who act in a socially responsible manner, understand the news media, and know how to achieve win-win outcomes in their media relations. The opportunities for positive interviews are abundant, indeed.

Perhaps a person's view of the world tells us more about the person than it does about the world.

Reading List

The books on this reading list are worth investigating to learn what others have to say on topics that apply directly or indirectly to news-media interviews and appearances. Some of the titles listed here express views that differ from those found in this book. I hope you explore these books and watch for additional titles in this evolving field.

News Media

Brush, Douglas P., and Brush, Judith M., *Private Television Communications into the Eighties (The Third Brush Report)* (Berkeley Heights, NJ: International Television Association, 1981).

Caruba, Alan, ed., *Power Media "Selects"* (Washington, DC: Broadcast Interview Source, 1989).

Davis, Mitchell P., ed., *Talk Show "Selects"* (Washington, DC: Broadcast Interview Source, 1989).

Dilenschneider, Robert L., *Power and Influence* (New York: Prentice-Hall, 1990).

Powers, Ron, *The Newscasters* (New York: St. Martin's Press, 1977).

Interviews

Ailes, Roger (with Jon Kraushar), *You Are the Message* (Homewood, IL: Dow Jones–Irwin, 1988).

Bland, Michael, *The Executive's Guide to TV and Radio Appearances* (White Plains, NY: Knowledge Industry Publications, 1980).

Brady, John, *The Craft of Interviewing* (New York: First Vintage Books, 1977).

Martin, Dick, *The Executive's Guide to Handling a Press Interview* (New York: Pilot Books, 1977).

Mincer, Richard, and Mincer, Deanne, *The Talk Show Book* (New York: Facts on File, 1982).

Shafer, Ross, *Talk Show Guest Workshop* (4 Tapes & Instruction Manual), (Woodland Hills, California: Shafer Productions Inc., 1989).

Shales, Tom, *On the Air* (New York: Summit Books, 1982).

Presenting Information

Berg, Karen, and Gilman, Andrew (with Edward P. Stevenson), *Get to the Point* (New York: Bantam Books, 1989).

Bowling, Evelyn Burge, *Voice Power* (Harrisburg, PA: Stackpole Books, 1980).

Frank, Milo, *How to Get Your Point across in 30 Seconds or Less* (New York: Simon & Schuster, 1986).

Greene, Alan, *The New Voice—How to Sing and Speak Properly* (Milwaukee, Wisconsin: Hal Leonard Publishing Corporation, [no date]).

Janes Hindman, Larry Kirkman, and Elizabeth Monk, *TV Acting: A Manual for Camera Performance* (New York: Hastings House, 1982).

Kemp, Jerrold E., *Planning and Producing Audiovisual Materials* (New York: Harper & Row, 1980).

Meuse, Leonard F., *Succeeding at Business and Technical Presentations* (New York: Wiley, 1988).

Miller, Sherod, Wackman, Daniel, Elam Nunnally, and Carol Saline, *Straight Talk* (New York: Rawson, Wade, 1981).

Rafe, Stephen C., *How to Be Prepared to Think on Your Feet and Give the Best Business Presentations of Your Life* (New York: HarperBusiness, 1990).

Walters, Dottie, and Lillet Walters, *Speak and Grow Rich* (Englewood Cliffs, NJ: Prentice-Hall, 1989).

Wilder, Lilyan, *Professionally Speaking* (New York: Simon & Schuster, 1986).

Managing Stress

Green, Elmer and Green, Alyce, *Beyond Biofeedback* (New York: Dell, 1977).

Tanner, Ogden, *Stress* (New York: Time-Life Books, 1976).

Uris, Auren, and Tarrant, Jack, *How to Keep from Getting Fired* (Chicago: Regnery, 1975).

Communications and Behavior

Bolton, Robert, *People Skills* (Englewood Cliffs, NJ: Prentice-Hall, 1979).

Comstock, George, Steven Chaffee, Natan Katzman, Maxwell McCombs, and Donald Roberts, *Television and Human Behavior* (New York: Columbia University Press, 1978).

Nierenberg, Gerald I., and Calero, Henry H., *Meta-Talk* (New York: Simon & Schuster, 1973).

Thompson, David S., *Language* (New York: Time-Life, 1975).

Weintraub, Walter, *Verbal Behavior, Adaptation and Psychopathology* (New York: Springer, 1981).

Nonverbal Communication

Ekman, Paul, *Telling Lies* (New York: Berkley Books, 1985).

Ekman, P., W. V. Friesen, and P. Ellsworth, *Emotion in the Human Face* (New York: Pergamon, 1972).

Morris, Desmond, *Manwatching* (New York: Abrams, 1977).

Nierenberg, Gerald I., and Calero, Henry H., *How to Read a Person Like a Book* (New York: Pocket Books, 1971).

Whiteside, Robert L., *Face Language* (New York: Pocket Books, 1974).

Marketing via Communication

Moine, Donald J., and Herd, John H., *Modern Persuasion Strategies* (Englewood Cliffs, NJ: Prentice-Hall, 1984).

Rein, Irving, Kotler, Philip, and Stoller, Martin, *High Visibility* (New York: Dodd, Mead, 1987).

Negotiating

Cohen, Herb, *You Can Negotiate Anything* (New York: Bantam Books, 1980).

Dawson, Roger, *You Can Get Anything You Want* (New York: Simon & Schuster, 1985).

Elgin, Suzette Haden, *The Gentle Art of Verbal Self-Defense* (Englewood Cliffs, NJ: Prentice-Hall, 1980).

Goffman, Erving, *Relations in Public* (London: Penguin, 1971).

Nierenberg, Gerald I., *the Art of Negotiating* (New York: Simon & Schuster, 1981).

Warschaw, Tessa Albert, *Winning by Negotiating* (New York: Berkley Books, 1980).

Neurolinguistic Programming

Many of the neurolinguistic programming (NLP) techniques developed by or used in the highly successful work of psychologists Milton Erickson and Virginia Satir (among others) are discussed in the following publications. More information on NLP publications is available from Real People Press, Box F, Moab, UT 84532, and Meta Publications, P.O. Box 565, Cupertino, CA 95014.

Bandler, Richard, *Magic in Action* (Cupertino, CA: Meta, 1985).

Bandler, Richard, and Grinder, John, *Frogs into Princes* (Moab, UT: Real People Press, 1979.

——— (Andreas, Steve and Connie, eds.), *Reframing* (Moab, UT: Real People Press, 1982).

———, *The Structure of Magic I* (Moab, UT: Real People Press, 1975).

Cameron-Bandler, Leslie, *They Lived Happily Ever After* (Cupertino, CA: Meta, 1978).

Dilts, Robert, *Applications of Neuro-Linguistic Programming,* Cupertino, CA, Meta Publications, 1983.

———, *Roots of Neuro-Linguistic Programming* (Cupertino, CA: Meta, 1983).

Dilts, Robert B., John Grinder, Richard Bandler, Judith DeLoaier, and Leslie Cameron-Bandler, *Neuro-Linguistic Programming I* (Cupertino, Ca: Meta, 1979).

Grinder, John, and Bandler, Richard, *The Structure of Magic II,* (Palo Alto, CA: Science and Behavior Books, 1976).

———, *Trance-formations* (Moab, UT: Real People Press, 1981).

Jacobson, Sid, *Meta-cation: Prescriptions for Some Ailing Educational Processes* (Cupertino, CA: Meta, 1983).

Richardson, Jerry, *The Magic of Rapport* (Cupertino, CA: Meta, 1987).

Robbins, Anthony, *Unlimited Power* (New York: Fawcett Colombine, 1986).

Yeager, Joseph, *A Collection of Articles on Management and NLP, 4th ed.* (Princeton, NJ: Eastern NLP Institute, 1985).

———, *Thinking about Thinking with NLP* (Cupertino, CA: Meta, 1985).

Index

161

Rapport Communications prepares people at all levels, in all fields, to present information and respond to questions effectively. Our methods help people make their points, gain acceptance in any situation, and achieve win-win outcomes—even under stress and regardless of the personalities involved.

Our seminars carry familiar titles:

Presentations. Public speaking, sales presentations, videotaped appearances, teleconferences, government testimony, management presentations, serving as "talent" on radio or television commercials or PSAs, editorial board briefings, and financial presentations (especially meetings of shareholders and security analysts).

Interviews. Talk shows, crisis response, news-media interviews (radio, television, and print), and executive-employment interviews.

Writing. Speechwriting for professionals, speechwriting for non-professionals, and feature-articles writing.

Each program can be custom-designed according to your priorities to include the instructional units you select and even combine various seminar formats. Programs can also be designed to employ your issues and your content exclusively.

In all its programs, Rapport Communications employs state-of-the-art techniques for teaching adults. As a result, participants learn new information rapidly, retain it well, and recall it when they need it most.

For information on Rapport seminars available to you or your organization, drop us a note. We would be pleased to show you how our services can help you or members of your organization communicate effectively in any environment.

Stephen C. Rafe, APR, President
Rapport Communications
Dept. HRB P. O. Box 3119
Warrenton, VA 22186
(703) 349-1039